Seeking
The Savior

by

Michael L. Kilday

Published by
New Generation Beat Publications

Copyright 2025
by
New Generation Beat Publications
and
Michael L. Kilday

All Rights Reserved

ISBN: 978-1-957654-23-2

Debbie Tosun Kilday - Editing & Cover Design.

Human Error Publishing - Editing & Formatting

New Generation Beat Publications asks that no part of this publication be reproduced or transmitted in any form or by any means electronic or mechanical, including photocopy, recording or information storage or retrieval system without permission in writing from Michael L. Kilday and New Generation Beat Publications. The reasons for this are to help support publisher and the artists.

DEDICATION

"Those in power write the history, while those who suffer write the songs". This was a quote from Irish songwriter Frank Harte anyone who gets rear-ended by history on a regular basis could appreciate.

A NOTE FROM THE AUTHOR

Over the millennia, too many untruths, half-truths, and outright lies have been told about the messiah, his life and his mission. This has led to the creation of a Faith based upon misconceptions, suppositions, and innuendo, effectively gaslighting the faithful. My intent was and always has been to reveal the practices used to propagate the Faith as outright lying, manipulation of reality, scapegoating, and coercion. My heartfelt desire was to make every effort to totally dispel them. In short, this book was written to reveal the historical speculations about Christianity, its origins and principles, the individuals who founded it, and extrapolate upon them. Furthermore, it will fulfill a personal destiny.

In 1979, my first deep trance session occurred with Elwood Babbitt of Wendell Depot, Massachusetts. At the time, he lived at a farm on the top of Northfield mountain. This session was detailed in my first book, TRUTH NEVER CHANGES: EARTH CHANGES, published in 2009. It featured predictions of global upheaval in the form of climatic disturbances, floods in the east and fires in the west, tornadoes all year round in the heartland, temperature fluctuations, catastrophic sea level rise, and a predicted pole shift. In addition, it placed humanity in a moral, spiritual, and societal vice grip that was ever tightening until the timer on REVELATION popped. Originally it was thought these changes were earmarked for 2012 because of a misinterpretation regarding the Mayan Calendar, but that year came and went without a final resolution to predictions of REVELATION. The prognostications have been rerouted to the early part of the 21st century as Edgar Cayce had originally predicted. Because prophecies are fulfilled when conditions are met rather than dates on calendars are reached, the prognosticator's timer still has yet to pop.

Thus the term 'Earth Changes' aptly fit the content of that aforementioned book which could be considered a warning to future generations that humanity was an endangered species, and the Earth it inhabited was endangered as well. These issues and concerns were what confronted humanity in the first half of the 21st century. This manuscript was an in-depth discussion of the impact of Earth Changes upon humanity in psychological, religious, psychic, societal and physical terms. These matters should not to be taken lightly or ignored because the survival of the human race was in the balance. Whether or not the term 'End Times' should be applied to any of these opinions or events as the Evangelicals and assorted cults were accustomed to doing could not be simply accepted or denied on the face of the allegation. It was rather a matter for debate because there were no simple problems or solutions. Instead they promised to be exceedingly complex. As the Doomsday Clock ticked forward, it seemed to be an acknowledgement from the powers that be that the problems were unsolvable.

The main reason for writing SEEKING THE SAVIOR surfaced in 1980. That was after a second deep trance session with Elwood Babbitt which took more of a personal turn in the subject matter conveyed. During that deep trance session, Spirit identified a short list of personalities with whom I had been affiliated throughout my 29 lifetimes. Of the several names provided, one name caught my attention, Philo of Alexandria. *"I see you in the Library at Alexandria"*, Spirit noted at one point in the session, *"where you are in the midst of study and contemplation; for you have always been in the pursuit of new beginnings and new experiences. There you have performed for if it was not true, the thought would not have entered your consciousness".*

At the time it was presented I had no clue who this personality was, but resolved to find out. Soon after the search began for the reason for its discovery at that time, how it was significant, and where it would lead. As I researched him, however, it became clear why it was presented to me at that time. Philo was a Jewish scholar, theologian, and historian who lived in Alexandria, Egypt during the first century of the common era. He wrote voluminously about Moses, and Hebrew scriptural exegesis comparing it to and contrasting it with Greek stoicism. He also wrote about his encounters with the Essene tribe living in Alexandria. A quantity of this material survived to the present day which I acquired and read a portion of it. To be honest, it was his connection to the Essene which was of particular interest to me.

In the mid-1980s when I became aware of the discovery of the Dead Sea Scrolls in Qumran, Jordan and the Coptic Christian codices in Nag Hammadi, Egypt, I reviewed a substantial number of those texts as well. Intrigued by their contents, I began to seriously reevaluate the origins of Christianity. I also began to recognize Philo's historical significance when I cross-referenced his segments on the Essene with the Dead Sea Scrolls and Coptic literature. Philo handled the material with a journalistic flare. Although I never considered myself an expert on the subject matter, I found it to be enlightening and thought provoking. It seemed to offer a unique perspective on the role of Essene Judaism in the development of the theologies of Western Civilization. I also found correlations in Essene Doctrine with the credo of the Great White Brotherhood and the Children of the Law of One which made me think these groups were interconnected. Furthermore it was quite possible the torch was passed from one to the other at appropriate times in the history of humankind.

Additionally, Philo of Alexandria was a contemporary of the man known as Jesus of Nazareth. Though he never wrote about him unless that material did not survive, he was in a position nonetheless to be one who stood at the crossroads of history, in much of the same way that the Jewish historian Josephus did. Today Philo was acknowledged as a primary source of information about the Jewish cultural phenomenon known as the Essene tribe. He actually knew them and documented his encounters with them in Alexandria. In an historical sense, he also served as a vital link between Judaism, the Jewish prophets, the Palestinian Church, and Gnosticism. He represented a vital thread running through the early years of the Judeo-Christian experience.

As the manuscript I was preparing began to take shape, it evidenced a directed flow in the development of Christian culture and theology throughout the first four centuries of the common era and beyond. In the Essene communal literature, one item was key to my analysis of historical events. It concerned the Jewish Messiah as an essential element of the Hebrew cultural heritage. It was noteworthy that the ruling class of the twelve tribes of Israel did not claim The Nazarene as one of their own. Instead the Sadducees and Pharisees conspired with the Romns to crucify him. One reason could be that the messianic component of that cultural heritage came from the Essene tribe. The exposition of that legacy came from the Jewish prophets, all of which, were sent forth by the Essene to preach in the Roman province of Judea. The relationship of the prophets and the people they preached to was not always cordial. It was recorded that there were times when the people railed against certain prophets. The fact that bits and pieces of the books of the Jewish prophets were found in the ruins of the Qumran settlement fortified the argument that the Essene settlements were the launching pad for the Jewish prophets. The salient point to note was that the man labelled as The Nazarene could be considered to be the last of those Jewish prophets. Therefore, it followed that if the Essene educated, trained, and sent all the other prophets into the world, then it was only logical to assume that they must have sent the last one too.

However the crux of the matter to be discovered, interrogated, and finally determined was the identity of the Essene's Teacher of Righteousness cited in the Dead Sea Scrolls. Was that teacher the messiah as well or was that a separate and distinct personality? The case could be made that Yeshua bar Yosef, also known as The Nazarene, fit that designation. Among other things, this manuscript was an attempt to discover exactly who that was, and if the man known to the world as The Nazarene was indeed the Teacher of Righteousness. If he was as I suspected, that personage, it would cast a spotlight upon the Essene tradition, and what it actually meant in real terms to the history of humankind. Moreover it would alter the historical record on the origins of Christianity, and indicate its true import for future generations. Whatever that may prove to be, it was probable that the authorities of the Christian religion were not likely to endorse that finding. It was probable they would instead deny there was a connection.

As far as I could imagine, this manuscript was my attempt to complete a study begun in the first century of the common era. But it could mean so much more when put in the proper framework and broadened in scope. For it would be appropriate to say that the past, present and future formulation of the spiritual mission of the Christ personality began long before this particular incarnation walked the Earth, and will continue long after he died. Instead of being tagged as the proverbial Son of God as the Orthodox Christians of Rome did, the reality was Yeshua bar Yosef was one in a line of succession of messiahs embodying the Christ Consciousness.

However, this Christ was not a one-off. Instead he was a chart member of the Great White Brotherhood from whose ranks the messiahs have always come to point humanity toward the Light. Until such time when it was not necessary for saviors to exist any longer, the path was 'walked' periodically. Over the course of Time, I have come to realize there have been many Christs and many missions, and it was my hope this manuscript will validate that point. Moreover it begged the question, what comes next?

Table 0f Contents

Chapter 1 The Argument	14
Chapter 2 The Birth Of Yeshua	19
Chapter 3 The Man, Yeshua	27
Chapter 4 The Man, Apollonius	35
Chapter 5 Philo Of Alexandria	45
Chapter 6 A Little Biblical Sleight Of Hand	52
Chapter 7 The Essene	63
Chapter 8 The Nag Hammadi Library	77
Chapter 9 The Descent To Untruth	85
Chapter 10 The Issue Of Gnosis	89
Chapter 11 The Propagation Of The Faith	103
Chapter 12 Sin And Absolution	113
Chapter 13 The Role Of Women In Gnosticism	124
Chapter 14 The Issue Of Martyrdom	138
Chapter 15 The Politics Of Power	144
Chapter 16 The Nicene Creed	152
Chapter 17 Monophystism Versus Dyophystism	162
Chapter 18 Gnostics In The Crosshairs	167
Chapter 19 The Battleground Of Doctrine	174
Chapter 20 The Legacy Of The Media Merchant	189
Chapter 21 Christ, The Traveler	200
Chapter 22 The Mission Of Yeshua The Christ	214
Chapter 23 The Children Of The Law Of One	228
Chapter 24 Applying The Law Of ONE	247
Chapter 25 Opening A Vista On The True Faith	256
Chapter 26 The Transition Of The Ages	267
Chapter 27 Conclusion	284
Chapter 28 Monolog	294
Chapter 29 Epilog	309
Bibliography	314

Chapter 1 The Argument

From the outset, I would like to state that this book did not propose a rejection of Christianity or its teachings. Its intention was to separate the Christ from the cultural expression called Catholicism which evolved from a political attachment to his teachings. In my opinion, a rejection of Christianity as it was practiced by traditional Christians was not a rejection of the one who became the Christ. It was instead the recognition that the man they worshipped as the messiah may not have been who they said he was, or that they made him out to be something he was not for their own purposes.

The proposition was: the Roman Catholic Church utilized the alias or pseudonym of *Jesus* to ensure the fictionalized accounts of the life of the Christ and his teachings would take on a life of its own, and become the historical record. It was my contention the tenets of this Church were not a true representation of his teachings. These historical contrivances contributed to the fiction that the canon of the Universal Church was the basis for the faith the Christ preached. However, my belief was the actual origin for this faith was an Essene belief system which flourished in the first century of the Common Era (CE) in the Middle East.

The culmination of its expression was the doctrine of THE CHILDREN OF THE LAW OF ONE which appeared in the first few centuries of the Common Era in Tibet. Furthermore, I believed it will be shown that the Essene connection to Christianity was a valid one because the Christ himself was quite literally a product of the Essene tribe. That topic will be addressed more fully in subsequent chapters.

Certainly the Universal Church exposed itself as an unholy alliance with the prevailing ideological and imperial power structures of the day. Furthermore, an accurate assessment of the historical record will show this to anyone who wished to investigate it. It will be demonstrated that the historical record which has come down to the present day has been purposefully manipulated to suggest the uniformity of Christian doctrine from its inception. However, it was anything else but that. This contrived historical record proposed that the Orthodox Christian brand was the only legitimate version of Christianity like it was a foregone conclusion rather than a calculated outcome. Orthodox Christians would be defined as those who believed the Synoptic gospels were the only records of the origin and rise of Christianity. However, when one sect systematically slashed and burned the entirety of the competing historical records found, humanity was left with the remains. It presented an incomplete and distorted depiction of the past.

Furthermore, the founders of the Universal Church proposed Christianity was centered in Rome. However, that was a subject for debate. In the first three centuries of the Common Era, homegrown versions of Christianity, popped up in Jerusalem, Syria, Persia, Greece, North Africa, and Egypt to name a few locales. Once this narrative proceeded to an examination of Gnosticism, it will be shown that the version of Christianity that arose in each one of these locales was as legitimate as the version of Christianity begun in Rome. Primarily this was because during the incident known as the Pentecost, the Apostles were charged to go throughout the known world and spread the Word. All things being equal, the source of the teaching which each apostle spread was the same. How it evolved from that point on was obviously not.

Since Simon Peter, the traditional leader of the Apostles, traveled to Rome, it was assumed that Rome was accorded a special place in the hierarchy of missionary destinations. That supposition was founded upon a gospel verse which noted Peter was the rock upon which Jesus would build the Church (*Matthew 16: 18-19*). The authorities of the early Church made that happen for reasons of their own. It could be argued, however, that Rome's vaunted position of papal authority was assumed because it was the seat of a global empire. By the fourth century of the Common Era, the purpose of the mission of the Universal Church then became to administer its authority in the subject kingdoms of the empire. Therefore, the assignment of Rome's status was a matter of convenience for efficiency of operation in the fulfillment of a theological manifest destiny, namely the Holy Roman Empire.

In the course of the text, it will be shown that the compilation of the historical record may have gotten many things wrong along the way for a variety of reasons. Some of those reasons were intentional, some were unintentional, but none of them were obvious, and all of them were debatable. Debate flourished in an environment where few historical records were kept, and those that survived were hotly contested. Reasonable doubt was appropriate while the jury was in deliberation. At the end of that deliberation a verdict will be reached. A salient point of contention was what it always has been: who were the scribes of the early Universal Church? What was their intent, and did they have an agenda? Was their claim that Scripture was the Word of God a valid proposition or was it simply the reflections of pious men? The Silence provided no answer, therefore the debate raged on.

At the very least, every Christian should question whether or not the history of their religion that they have been force-fed throughout their entire lives has been fabricated to suit the needs and desires of the powers-that-be in the church of their choosing. What needed to happen now was a new inquiry into the historical record so that it could be re-examined for all to see, and let the chips fall where they may. The 20th century discoveries of the DEAD SEA SCROLLS and NAG HAMMADI codices made the present moment in time the appropriate juncture to ask those probing questions of the powers-that-be in the Universal Church. Specifically, they were: what did they know, when did they know it, and what were they going to do about it? As a result of the soul-searching one question remained: Was it time to disclose the truth about their prophet?

Chapter 2 The Birth Of Yeshua

Recent research suggested the full name of the Christ also known as Jesus of Nazareth, was Y'shua bar Yosef. The derivation of his historical name was as follows: the name Yeshua came from the Aramaic language, and the name Yoshua came from the Hebrew language, which was an alternative form of Yehoshua with the English translation being Joshua. In Hebrew it meant *may Jehovah help him*. The name Jesus came from the Greek form, Iesous. It meant *hail Zeus* or *God is salvation*. Given all the variations of his name, it may cause confusion, but they all refer to the same person. According to recent research, the name Jesus was simply the Greek translation of the Hebrew man, Y'shua bar Yosef. Therefore logic dictated wherever the name Jesus was referenced, it substituted for that historical individual.

All things considered, this person might be the one individual in history who everyone wanted to believe they knew intimately, but in reality, they knew very little about. Primarily what the general public today knew of was his ministry which lasted approximately 5 years. What they did not know was: who he really was, where he came from, who his family was, and the bulk of the circumstances of his actual life before he was 30 years of age. Therefore, the stories about him abounded to fill in the blanks, and in all probability, the stories might be fiction. Throughout this text, his Aramaic name was used primarily because according to the historians, that was the language he spoke. Therefore, Yeshua was the name his parents gave him.

The date of Yeshua's birth on April 17, 6 BCE, was corroborated by the appearance of the Star of Bethlehem in the night sky over Judea or Judaea as the Romans called it. That astrological event should be reason enough to fix the date of his birth in Bethlehem in the Roman province of Judaea on that day. Technically Synoptic gospel tradition, meaning the gospels of Matthew, Mark, and Luke, gave no precise date for his birth. Because in those days calendars were scarce, they simply associated his birth with the Star of Bethlehem. The fourth gospel written by John concentrated primarily on the theology and mission of the Christ, and did not include as many details of his life story as the other three gospels.

The Synoptic gospels asserted that Yeshua was born during the reign of Augustus Caesar. If that assertion was correct, that would provide a range for a tentative birth date anywhere between 27 BCE and 14 CE. After Yeshua's death, the assignment of the date of 1 CE for the birth of the Christ was always an assumption made after the fact because no definitive date was recorded. Therefore, rather than the powers-that-be of the Universal Church having to admit they did not know when he was born, a date was arbitrarily assigned to his birth. Consequently, having an actual date now in 6 BCE, set the stage as it should be for the entrance of the Christ onto the world stage.

The Star of Bethlehem was believed to be a planetary alignment that caught the attention of the Persian Magi. It may have been intellectual curiosity that prompted their visit, rather than their visit being a religious pilgrimage. In the Catholic religion, this visit had been celebrated annually on January 6th as The Epiphany. A recent theory suggested that their attention related directly to a prediction Zoroaster had made 1000 years earlier that the spirit of God would return to Earth foretold by a spectacular astrological aspect. What Zoroaster had to say was profoundly significant because he was widely acknowledged as the immediately previous incarnation of the Christ. More or less his word was the equivalent of the word of God to his followers. It was reasonable to assume that Zoroaster's prediction was what brought the Magi to Bethlehem, since at this late date one could not possibly know their motivation. Though it was a reasonable assumption.

Apparently, the Magi felt the need to make the trek to Bethlehem to greet the new Christ, and so the story goes they brought gifts with them fit for a king. However, if they had thought for a moment about the circumstances of Yeshua's birth, the gifts they chose would have been other than frankincense, myrrh and gold. He was not making an entrance as a rich man, but rather as a pauper. It was a foreshadowing of his prophetic mission that few to this day really seemed to fully grasp the purpose of, and they showed that in how they celebrated their faith, particularly those of the evangelical variety.

For example, a prosperity gospel was the current rage, but it would be safe to say that Yeshua would not approve of that gospel. He would contend spiritual riches like love, peace, and the brotherhood of Man were what brought God into one's life, rather than the gaudy opulence displayed by material wealth and prosperity. He did not clear the temple in Jerusalem of the money changers on a whim. In his view, they were desecrating sacred ground, treating the Temple in Jerusalem like it was a commercial enterprise. His response was to cast them out with extreme prejudice.

Yeshua would not hesitate to do the same today. In modern times, the very same gaudy opulence and Cha-ching of the cash register continued to plague the expression of religious practices of all types. In a heartbeat, Yeshua would clear the sacristy of the scourge of the moneychangers again if given the opportunity. Embracing the prosperity gospel was a stain upon the religious faith of the false prophets, though the offenders would never see it that way. In God's realm, however, sharing was preferred over hoarding, darkness fled before the light, the lie shriveled in the face of the truth, so the story goes.

According to an article in the South Bend Tribune on December 8th, 2013, Grant Matthews, professor of theoretical astrophysics and cosmology in the Department of Physics at the University of Notre Dame's College of Science, had been studying the Star of Bethlehem for over a decade. After studying historical, astronomical and biblical records, Matthews proposed that the event that led the Magi to Bethlehem was a rare planetary alignment that occurred in the year of 6 BCE. During the alignment, the sun, Jupiter, the moon and Saturn were all in Aries. According to Matthews, while Venus was situated in Pisces, Mercury and

Mars were situated in Taurus. At the time, Aries was also the location of the vernal equinox. The significance of the appearance of a sign in the sky at Yeshua's birth was that it substantiated the gospel birth story. The questions to be answered, if they could be definitively answered were: what was the purpose of the sign, and was it a sign, or a cosmic coincidence?

Matthews' research noted that the presence of Jupiter and the moon signified the birth of a ruler with a special destiny. Saturn was a symbol of the giving of life, as was the presence of Aries in the vernal equinox, also marking the start of spring. The professor alleged that alignment in Aries signified a newborn ruler in Judea to the Magi who were Zoroastrian priests from ancient Babylon and Mesopotamia. It will be 16,000 years before a similar alignment will be seen again, according to Matthews' calculations, and then the vernal equinox will not be in Aries. Mathews said he could not find an alignment like the one known as the Bethlehem Star going out as far as the next 500,000 years. Therefore, the singularity of this event signified its magnitude, the import of which would have an everlasting impact upon the world. Apparently, that was pretty much how the Magi saw it, and they acted accordingly.

The Roman Catholic Church had alleged for centuries that Jesus of Nazareth was crucified on the first full-day of Passover Friday April 7, 30 CE or 7/4/782 AUC by the Roman calendar. This meant that the Christ was 34-years-old at the time of his death and would have turned 35 ten days later. The significance of his death and resurrection during the Jewish celebration of Passover in and of itself had a profound significance. It served as a marker in the tribal race memory indicating liberation and rebirth. That liberation inferred a release from the metaphorical slavery of material bonds, with the rebirth culminating in the resurrection of the Spirit in a new covenant of Faith with the Deity. Theoretically this correlated with the Hebrews escaping from bondage in Egypt to the Promised Land under the guidance of Moses.

It was worthy to note, if Yeshua was a fictional character, how could so many Orthodox and Gnostic Christians be deceived into thinking he was an actual person? It defied logic that a subterfuge of this magnitude could persist for millennia. Certainly, his teachings had a source, and most likely there was a historical personage that carried the mantle of these teachings. The clues to their origin could be traced to the Essene living in Alexandria, Egypt in the first century of the Common Era, and their one known biographer, Philo of Alexandria. That will be addressed in a subsequent chapter. In the next chapter, the personage known as Y'shua bar Yosef will be presented to provide some historical context for the ensuing discussion.

Chapter 3 The Man, Yeshua

Whether or not Yeshua was an actual historical person had been a matter of debate in some circles of modern scholarship for the past century. In the historical records that survived to the present day from antiquity, other than the canonical gospels of Matthew, Mark, Luke, and John, there was nary a mention of him. This was significant because other than the records of the Universal Church, there was very little corroborating evidence that Yeshua, aka Jesus of Nazareth, even existed. Furthermore, it was corroborating evidence that often validated the historical record. Thus, finding corroborating evidence was critical to establishing historical identity.

Except for two historians in the first century of the Common Era who allegedly were his contemporaries, Yeshua was an unknown quantity to those who did not know him. These historians were: Josephus, a Jewish historian, who wrote volumes on the history of the Jews, and the Jewish ex-patriot historian and theologian Philo of Alexandria who wrote extensively on Moses and the Essene living in Alexandria, Egypt. Neither the names Yeshua nor Jesus were mentioned in Philo's work, and the name Jesus was only briefly mentioned in the work of Josephus. Because of the audience to which his work was directed, Josephus used the Greek derivation of Yeshua's name. Furthermore, because the Synoptic gospels were initially written in Greek rather than Aramaic, it was understandable that the name of Jesus rather than Yeshua was carried forward into common Biblical usage.

Flavius Josephus lived in Judea, circa 37 CE to 100 CE. He was close to being a contemporary of the Christ, a Jewish historian and military leader who was born in Jerusalem to a father of priestly descent, and a mother who claimed royal ancestry. He was best known for his work, THE JEWISH WAR, which chronicled the Jewish rebellion against Roman rule from 66 to 70 CE which ended in the siege of Masada. He also wrote ANTIQUITIES OF THE JEWS which detailed the history of the world from a Jewish perspective for a Greek and Roman audience. The Jewish revolt in which he took part as head of the Jewish forces in Galilee, raged for five years. In 69 CE, Josephus defected to the Roman side of the conflict, and was granted his freedom by the emperor Vespasian at which time Josephus assumed the emperor's family name of Flavius.

In addition to the Bible, the works of Josephus were the chief source of information for the history of ancient

Judea. They provided vital insight into first century Judaism, its main events, and the background of early Christianity. They also provided an independent account of historical figures such as Pontius Pilate, Herod the Great, John the Baptist, James the Just, and Philo of Alexandria. Whether or not the opinion of a traitor to his own people could be trusted to give an accurate historical account of his own people was a valid point. However, without knowing the man, Josephus, or the circumstances of his treachery, one had to leave it at that, and simply accept what he wrote without judgment and assume it was accurate. Moreover, it was highly unlikely that Josephus would have written any histories of the Jews had he not defected to the Romans during the Jewish revolt. Given the outcome of the revolt, it was probable he would not have survived it. Therefore, his treachery had a purpose and produced a historical record that would not have otherwise existed. That was the salient point to be noted. Concerning the person called Jesus, *he* wrote.

> *Now there was about this time Jesus, a wise man, if it be lawful to call him a man; for he was a doer of wonderful works, a teacher of such men as receive the truth with pleasure. He drew over to him both many of the Jews and many of the Gentiles. He was [the] Christ. And when Pilate, at the suggestion of the principal men amongst us [the Sanhedrin and Roman authorities], had condemned him to the cross, those*

> that loved him at the first did not forsake him; for he appeared to them alive again the third day; as the divine prophets had foretold these and ten thousand other wonderful things concerning him. And the tribe of Christians so named after him are not extinct at this day.

Both Josephus and Philo were contemporaries of a Hebrew man named Y'shua bar Yosef, and they wrote extensively about the cultural history of the Jewish people. By today's reckoning, it was unthinkable that a person of Yeshua's stature and impact would not have been mentioned in Jewish history. Supposedly he figured prominently in it. He even deserved a mention in Roman history, specifically in reference to events as recorded circa 30 CE in Jerusalem.

Although it appeared Philo was not aware of Yeshua's existence, he was also probably aware a Teacher of Righteousness was cited in the Essene communal literature. No name was ever officially attached to that designation. However, if Yeshua was that aforementioned teacher, it bestowed upon him the pedigree to be listed among Melchizedek's stable of Hebrew prophets. Certainly, Yeshua fit that description in practice and principle because he was an Essene by birth. His parents, Mary and Joseph (or Yosef), were reputed to be Essene as was his Uncle Zachariah and Aunt Anna who were the parents of John the

Baptist. Since Jewish tribal membership was determined primarily by familial association, and Mary and Anna were reputed to be sisters, it was logical to believe the entire family was members of the Essene tribe.

Furthermore, Yeshua's aunt and uncle resided in Alexandria, Egypt. Therefore, it was reasonable to assume that Philo may have made acquaintance with them since the individuals in question were prominent in the Jewish community of the day as was Philo. Though Philo did not mention them by name in his study of the Essene tribe, and it should be noted he usually did not include names in his writings, except for Moses, one could assume they knew each other. It would be difficult to believe they would not have encountered each other at some point in their lives.

If Yeshua had been profiled in PLUTARCH'S LIVES, today there could be no doubt he was a historical personage. It would be case closed on that subject. Plutarch, circa 45 to 120 CE, was born a decade or so after Yeshua's death. Even though Plutarch wrote primarily about prominent Greeks and Romans of the era, one must still wonder why he did not include Yeshua, aka Jesus of Nazareth, in his biographies. If one considered how influential his teachings turned out to be for succeeding generations and his impact upon the future Roman Empire, he would be prime subject matter. But then again there was no social media in those days. Word traveled slowly and there was no nightly news, or it was all much ado about nothing; meaning the life of Jesus of Nazareth was all an elaborate fictionalized account. One could imagine the reason why Yeshua was never profiled was because the erasure of Essene culture was so complete after Masada. Their disappearance from the historical landscape of the Middle East was nearly absolute, almost as if it was by design.

Additionally, Judea was a backwater Roman province which had little influence upon the prevailing cultural disposition of the Empire. Judea did not have the stature of Rome, Greece, Egypt or Persia so it commanded little respect globally as a locale. It was likely little attention was paid to what happened there by Romans, Greeks, Egyptians, or Persians unless events dictated it. For example, the Jewish tax revolt of 66 CE was one such event when the Roman authorities would have taken notice. It was fairly obvious that the powers-that-be in the Roman world did not care much what happened there unless it had a direct impact upon their political authority. Certainly, a rebellion against Roman authority was worth mentioning in the annals of Roman history. It was a challenge to Roman authority in the region that was brutally suppressed by Roman legions. From the Roman point of view, little else the Jews did warranted any mention in the greater scheme of things. Apparently, that included a Jewish prophet born in Bethlehem who caused a stir in Jerusalem in the Roman province of Judaea circa 30 CE. Curiously that did not generate much more than a footnote in the history of the Roman Empire.

On the other hand, there was another person in the mix whose followers in the first century of the Common Era claimed had the pedigree to be recognized as a prominent prophet, philosopher, and seer with metaphysical leanings. He was a Greek philosopher who many of his followers claimed was a competitor for the title of the messiah and savior of humanity. His name was Apollonius of Tyana, a contemporary of Yeshua. The tales told about these two men implied they were interchangeable, and often gave rise to reasonable doubt about who was who. This confusion was certainly not something which Apollonius or Yeshua intended to happen. There was no evidence to support that either man was ever consciously competing with the other in any manner, shape, or form. It was possible neither man was even aware of the other's existence.

However as was often the case with celebrities, it was the celebrity worshippers who determined how they were treated over the course of their lives, and how celebrities were remembered after they passed. For the most part despite who Yeshua and Apollonius were and what they may have accomplished in their individual lives, the historical record was out of their hands. It was not written by them. One might say both men were captives of their own celebrity. How they were remembered was the reflection of the stories written about them. Whether or not those tales were written by men who knew them was entirely a matter of conjecture. In many cases, however, it was obvious they were not. Thus their lives very well may have been the stuff of legend, and had little to do with reality. How it came about that Apollonius would be associated with and/or confused with Yeshua will be explained in the next chapter.

Chapter 4 The Man, Apollonius

Apollonius of Tyana was born into a respected and wealthy Greek family in the town of Tyana in the Roman province of Cappadocia in Anatolia, now known as Turkey. He was a Greek Neo-Pythagorean philosopher. Although the precise dates of his birth and death were uncertain, most scholars agreed that he was a contemporary of the man called Jesus of Nazareth. His primary biographer, Philostratus the Elder, circa 170 to 247 CE, gave the timeline of Apollonius as circa 3 BCE to 97 CE. The book he wrote was entitled THE LIFE OF APOLLONIUS OF TYANA, a lengthy, novelistic biography, written at the request of Empress Julia Domna. She died in 217 CE, and he completed it soon after her death.

Philostratus described Apollonius as a wandering teacher of philosophy and miracle-worker who was active mainly in Greece and Asia Minor, but also traveled to Italy, Spain, North Africa, Mesopotamia, India, and Ethiopia. In particular, he told lengthy stories of Apollonius entering the city of Rome in disregard of Emperor Nero's ban on philosophers, and later on being summoned, as a defendant, to the court of Domitian, where he defied the emperor in blunt terms. He had allegedly been accused of conspiring against the emperor, performing human sacrifice, and predicting a plague by means of magic. Philostratus suggested that upon his death, Apollonius of Tyana underwent heavenly assumption while still alive. How that was accomplished was unknown, but it mirrored the so-called ascension of Yeshua to heaven after the celebration of Pentecost.

How much of this could be accepted as historical fact depended largely upon the extent to which modern scholars trusted the words of Philostratus, and in particular upon whether they believed in the veracity of his story. Some of these scholars contended that Apollonius never traveled to Western Europe. They claimed he was virtually unknown there until the 3rd century of the Common Era. It was then when Empress Julia Domna who was herself from the province of Syria decided to popularize him, and his teachings in Rome. For that purpose, so these same scholars believed, she commissioned Philostratus to write the biography, in which Apollonius was exalted as a fearless sage with supernatural powers, even greater than Pythagoras.

In his book, DID JESUS EXIST? THE HISTORICAL ARGUMENT FOR JESUS OF NAZARETH, Bart D. Ehrman described a figure from the first century of the Common Era. Ironically few realized the person he was writing about was Apollonius of Tyana. One would assume the following passage clearly described Yeshua, aka, Jesus of Nazareth. The passage seemed to describe him, but it was not written about him.

> *Even before he was born, it was known that he would be someone special. A supernatural being informed the mother the child she was to conceive would not be a mere mortal but would be divine. He was born miraculously, and he became an unusually precocious young man. As an adult he left home and went on an itiner ant preaching ministry, urging his listeners to live, not for the material things of this world, but for what is spiritual. He gathered a number of disciples around him, who became convinced that his teach ings were, divinely inspired, in no small part because he himself was divine. He proved it to them by doing many miracles, healing the sick, casting out demons, and raising the dead. But at the end of his life he roused opposition, and his enemies delivered him*

over to the Roman authorities for judgment. Still, after he left this world, he returned to meet his followers in order to convince them that he was not really dead but lived on in the heavenly realm. Later some of his followers wrote books about him.

Biblical scholar Bart D. Ehrman disclosed that in the introduction to his textbook on the New Testament, he described an important figure from the first century of the Common Era without first revealing he was writing about the stories featuring Apollonius of Tyana. Few Christians realized it would be so difficult to tell the two men apart. Similarities shared by the stories about the life of Apollonius and the life of Jesus of Nazareth included the following parallels detailed below.

They both had births that were miraculously announced by God. Both were religiously precocious as children. Both were asserted to be native speakers of Aramaic. Whereas Apollonius was known to have been influenced by Plato's philosophy, the Gnostic gospels suggested the teachings of Jesus of Nazareth reflected knowledge of Platonism. Both denounced wealth in their teachings, as well as renounced wealth in their lives. Both followed practices of abstinence and asceticism. Both wore long hair and robes. Both were reputed to be unmarried and childless. Both were anointed with oil. Both went to Jerusalem. Both taught in metaphors and parables. Both saw and predicted the future. Both healed the sick and performed miracles. Both cast out evil spirits and demons. Both raised the children of Roman and Jewish officials from the dead. Both spoke as a lawgiver. While Apollonius was on a mission to bring Greek culture to the barbarians, Jesus of Nazareth was on a mission to bring Christian culture to all the nations of the world. Both were reputed to be saviors from heaven. Both were accused of being magicians. Both were condemned by Roman authorities. While Apollonius was imprisoned in Rome, Jesus of Nazareth was imprisoned in Jerusalem. While Apollonius was assumed into heaven, Jesus of Nazareth ascended into heaven. Both appeared posthumously to detractors as a brilliant light. Both had their images revered in temples and churches respectively.

It was not difficult to imagine how these aforementioned attributes, applied to Apollonius, could just as easily be re-applied to a similar traveling teacher like Yeshua. Being contemporaries, the two men were philosophers who in spired all who encountered them, notwithstanding the philosophies they preached. One could easily be mistaken for the other or be substituted for the other in the public consciousness. Through the fog of Time, misappropriation of character, virtue, and deportment was inevitable. Since the fog was already thick regarding the remote past, it was understandable why the issue was confused.

Furthermore, it must be said about Apollonius that his existence had some factual basis as well, even though it was single-source. Moreover, it may very well be that Apollonius was the principal character of the fabled lost years of Jesus; he being the one who traveled the known world collecting the wisdom of the sages for the purpose of his education. For the purposes of consistency and coherence when those lost years were treated in the text, the name of Yeshua could be inserted instead of Apollonius or Jesus. The source from which the stories of the lost years were taken, THE AQUARIAN GOSPEL OF JESUS THE CHRIST, made an assumption that Jesus was the one who traveled through out the known world at the time. One could make a strong case for either man, but it was more likely, however, that the traveler was Apollonius of Tyana because logic dictated that was the more likely choice. However, at this late date, no one could be certain who it was. Therefore, any claim to know the identity of the traveler, the fabled St Issa, was pure speculation based upon a desire to make it so. This matter will be discussed in more detail later in the chapter called Christ, the Traveler.

Apollonius of Tyana, a contemporary of Yeshua, whose life was recorded by the Sophist Philostratus, was believed to be a carbon-copy of Yeshua by some scholars. The real question to be answered was whether Yeshua or Apollonius was the carbon-copy, or were they both separate and distinct historical figures? Apollonius like Yeshua was a traveling teacher who reportedly performed miracles and was believed to be a supernatural being in the flesh. His travels took him from one end of the known world to the other. In his travels, Apollonius accumulated all the knowledge of the local masters he visited. Along the way, he attained the acclaim of being regarded a learned philosopher and teacher in his own right. But then again Philostratus was the main source of all the information about Apollonius. In much the same way, the canonical gospels were the main source of all the information about Yeshua. In both cases, both histories came from single-source documentation with little or no corroboration from other contemporary sources. Therefore, it indicated that people were inclined to believe what they chose to believe. Whether or not it really happened, both tales still had all of the earmarks of a fable in either case. It was what hopes, wishes and dreams were made of, the same stuff as religion.

Ehrman implied from his research that the followers of Apollonius believed the person known as Jesus of Nazareth was a fabrication, while insisting Apollonius was a real person. Be that as it may, the question of which one was a historical figure or not will not be a subject of this book. It will be assumed he was. That conclusion will be based upon the few lines found in Josephus's ANTIQUITIES OF THE JEWS that suggested Yeshua's existence, under the Greek alias of Jesus, had some factual basis independent of the canonical gospels. The same will be assumed about Apollonius of Tyana, acknowledging the work of Philostratus was probably an accurate historical account. Their lives may or may not have intersected at some point, or they may or may not have known each other, no one can say for sure, especially at this late date. However, neither Yeshua nor Apollonius had the public relations apparatus of the Universal Church geared toward ensuring their lives would be remembered forever like Yeshua's under the moniker of Jesus. However, the details of Yeshua's life were itemized as the Universal Church wanted them to be, but probably not as they actually were as will be revealed later in this text.

Perhaps one just chalked it all up to semantics; in that, the Greek derivation of the Christ's given name prevailed, worldwide. And just because few took a close look at the derivation of the name until recently, no one had postulated the Christ's family connection with the Essene tribe, nor his time spent with the group in Alexandria. For millennia, it all quietly slipped under the radar. No one really noticed so nothing was said about it until after the discoveries of the DEAD SEA SCROLLS and the NAG HAMMADI codices in the 1940s.

Then the inquiries began in earnest about a great many aspects of the life of the Christ, and the people around him. Ultimately the trail led to Philo of Alexandria and his study of the Essene. His work was of key importance to understanding who Yeshua was, his legacy, his familial associations, and what his purpose on Earth might have been all along that was not common knowledge.

Chapter 5 Philo Of Alexandria

Philo Judaeus of Alexandria, who lived from 20 BCE to 50 CE, was a Hellenistic Jewish scholar and historian who wrote primarily about Moses. His deployment of allegory to harmonize Jewish scripture, mainly the Torah with Greek philosophy, was the first documented attempt of its kind, a marriage of Jewish exposition and Stoic philosophy. He was an expert in Jewish law and an interpreter of that law.

According to Josephus, Philo was inspired by Aristobulus of Alexandria who has been called the first Jewish theologian, circa 200 BCE to 145 BCE, who taught at the temple school in Alexandria. From him Philo was inspired to learn his trade as a prominent Biblical interpreter and theologian. Philo along with notable Jewish and Christian thinkers of his time like Athanasius, Origen, Cyril, Clement, and Aristobulus helped to shape the history of Biblical interpretation and theology. In the first few centuries of the Common Era, they helped to make Alexandria one of the intellectual capitals in the Roman world. The actual focal point of learning was the Library at Alexandria which was the centerpiece of scholarship for the region. It remained a vital cultural force in the region until at least the end of the 2nd century of the Common Era.

Because it was part of the history of the Roman Empire, the only event in Philo's life that could be documented and precisely dated was his participation in a trip to Rome in 40 CE. In that venture, he represented the Alexandrian Jews in a delegation to the Roman Emperor Gaius Caesar Augustus Germanicus who was known as Caligula. The delegation was sent to Rome following the civil strife between the Jewish and Greek communities in Alexandria.

As a contemporary of the Apostle Paul and Yeshua, Philo Judaeus was unquestionably an important historical figure for historians and students of Hellenistic Judaism and early Christianity. Although Philo did not explicitly mention Yeshua, or Paul, or any of the followers of Yeshua in his writings, he lived in their world. Philo did often describe the creative force of God as God's Logos like the apostle John. Whether or not Philo ever encountered Yeshua, The Teacher of Righteousness, was a matter of conjecture. No material survived that showed Philo wrote about it, and one would imagine he would have if he had ever met him. However, his expertise brought him into contact with the Essene tribe that operated in Alexandria, Egypt.

In his writings, he described the cultural behaviors and

character of the Essene community he encountered in Alexandria, including their customs and beliefs. It was important to note that Philo's writings of the Essene came from eye-witness accounts of his contact with the Alexandrian contingent of this group. From THE WORKS OF PHILO, these two selections came from the discourse called *On the Contemplative Life or Suppliants*. Philo wrote.

> *Having mentioned the Essenes, who in all respects selected for their admiration for the practical course of life, and who excel in all. Or what perhaps may be a less unpopular and invidious thing to say, in most of its parts, I will now proceed, in the regular order of my subjects, to speak of those who have embraced the speculative life...They are called the therapeutae and therapeutrides (healers) either because they profess an art of medicine more excellent than that in general use in cities (for that only heals bodies, but the other heals souls which are under the mastery of terrible and almost incurable diseases, which pleasures andappetites, fears and griefs, and covetousness, and follies, and injustice, and all the rest of the innumerable multitude for other passions and vices, have inflicted upon them), or else be cause they have been instructed by nature and the sacred laws to serve the living God, who is superior to the good, and more simple than the one and more ancient than the unit; with whom. However, who is there of those who rofess piety that we can possibly compare?*

Philo then went into a long discourse of how the Essene was different from the Greeks and Egyptians who worshipped graven images of stone. The latter also were infatuated with the physical life to the extent that they ignored the simple life of contemplation. He pointed out repeatedly that the Essene value system did not permit a fixation upon materialism. All things being equal it was not only a matter of education but character and values that spelled the difference in behavior. Furthermore the religious values of the Essene were totally different because their source doctrines were. That was what really set them apart from the pagans as well as the other Jewish tribes. It provided a perspective that the life of mind and soul were far more important than the acquisition of beautiful things and the appreciation of their grandeur. For the Essene, spirituality was a noteworthy virtue and the entire group shared that opinion. Their lives were proof of that. He wrote.

> *Therefore they [the Essene] always retain an imperishable recollection of God, so that not even in their dreams is any other object ever presented to their eyes except the beauty of the divine virtues and of the divine powers. Therefore many persons speak in their sleep, divulging and publishing the celebrated*

doctrines of the sacred philosophy and they are accustomed to pray twice each day at morning and at evening; when the sun is rising entreating God that the happiness of the coming day may be real happiness, so that their minds may be filled with Heavenly Light, and when the sun is setting they pray that their soul, being entirely lightened and relieved of the burden of the outward senses, and of the appropriate object of these outward senses, may be able to trace out truth existing in its own consistory and council chamber. And the interval between morning and evening is by them devoted wholly to meditation on and to practice of virtue, for they take up the sacred scriptures and philosophise concerning them, investigating the allegories of their national philosophy, since they look upon their literal expressions as symbols of some secret meaning of Nature, intended to be conveyed in those figurative expressions. They also have writings of ancient men, who having been the founders of one sect or another have left behind them many memorials of the allegorical system of writing and explanation, whom they take as a kind of model, and imitate the general fashion of their sect; so that they do not occupy themselves solely upon contemplation, but they likewise compose psalms and hymns to God in every kind of metre and melody imaginable, which they of necessity arrange in more dignified rhythm.

In great detail, Philo described the daily life of the Essene, the prayer vigils twice daily at morning and evening, the vegan dietary fare they ate daily except for festivals, and the regular meetings of contemplation. He laid out the daily routines in a journalistic fashion. Their monastic style of living dominated from morning to night, filled with periods devoted to the study of sacred scriptures as well as meditation. Philo could only be so detailed in his recording if he witnessed their activities. Being Jewish himself, Philo may have even participated in some of them.

He also noted *"they have also writings of ancient men, who having been the founders of one sect or another have left behind many memorials of the allegorical system of writing and explanation, whom they take as a kind of model, and imitate the general fashion of their sect."* Philo did not say specifically what the ancient writings were, but was probably referring to their substantial collection of communal literature. These would definitely include the writings of Enoch, Moses, as well as the Hebrew prophets. Since Philo was a great admirer of Moses, and had made a lifetime study of his work, that most likely drew his attention to the storehouse of written material the Essene possessed. In a subsequent chapter, the text went into greater detail on the subject of their communal literature of the Essene.

Chapter 6 A Little Biblical Sleight Of Hand

After reading the passages Philo wrote about the Essene, one thing was for certain, one received clear insight into how Yeshua's beliefs, mannerisms, and character were formed. Certainly Yeshua, aka Jesus of Nazareth, was not cast as the typical Hebrew peasant that would have spent his formative years living in a small village in Galilee. Considering the Essene influence, it became clearer how he could appear to be less Jewish in his beliefs, mannerisms, and character than the average Hebrew, and more like a Christian who espoused peace, love, and the brotherhood of Man. In other words, the perspective was more global and less tribal. It was more than a mode of evolution. It indicated the adoption of the Essene brand of Judaism which was his family's legacy.

Therefore when King Herod the Great of Judea ordered the execution of all male Hebrew children two years old and under in the vicinity of Bethlehem circa 4 BCE, it was noteworthy that Yeshua's family escaped to Alexandria, Egypt. It was as if they had forewarning of the danger Herod posed to the Christ child like they had a spy in Herod's court. Or perhaps the wise men stopped by and warned them on their return trip to Persia. Furthermore this option would not have been available to Yeshua's family, had not Mary's sister Anna lived in Alexandria, and was a prominent member of the Essene tribe.

In Scripture, King Herod's genocide was labelled the *Massacre of the Innocents.* Hence it was recorded in the Gospels which lent credence to the fact that Yeshua was indeed born in 6 BCE, not 1 CE as the Universal Church later proposed. The gospel of Matthew and history of the Jews written by Flavius Josephus confirmed the sequence of events. According to Flavius Josephus, Herod the Great died in 4 BCE. His pathological crusade to slaughter the male children of Israel had to have occurred about the time when the gospel of Matthew suggested it did. It only made sense.

Herod's psychopathic behavior was evidence of a regal sociopathic tendency verging on extreme paranoia. Herod's main concern was in preserving his royal line of succession. Essentially the new so-called king was viewed as a threat to it, or so he imagined. The gospels recorded this event causally as if a two-year-old child was actually a threat. *"Then Herod, when he saw that he was deceived by the wise men, was exceedingly angry; and he sent forth and put to death all the male children who were in Bethlehem and in all its districts, from two years old and under, according to the time which he had determined from the wise men" (Matthew 2: 16).* Of course, in any Age, a sane person would consider Herod's behavior to be the act of a delusional psychopath.

After fleeing from Herod's domain, the gospels suggested the family stayed in Egypt for six months. It was possible however Yeshua's family took Herod's massacre as a sign that their lives were in danger while he lived, and stayed in Egypt at least until Herod died later that year, or possibly much longer. Perhaps they stayed there until Yeshua was ready to embark upon his prophetic mission. All things considered that was just as likely a possibility as them having returned to Nazareth. There was no way to know for certain which was the more likely scenario after the fact.

These events bring into focus why the historical record was very sparse on Yeshua's proposed life in the town of Nazareth as a boy. It was conceivable that none of that happened. Perhaps it was all fabricated to fill in the blanks when the subject of his past life became an issue. There was one gospel story of his meeting with Jewish Pharisees and Sadducees to instruct them on interpreting

Jewish Law at twelve years old. The family had gone to Jerusalem for Passover and Yeshua stayed behind when his family had left. *"After three days they found him in the temple, sitting among the teachers, listening to them and asking them questions. And all who heard him were amazed at his understanding and his answers. And when his parents saw him, they were astonished. And his mother said to him, 'Son, why have you treated us so? Behold your father and I have been searching for you in great distress'. And he said to them, 'why were you looking for me? Did you not know that I must be in my father's house'?" (Luke 2: 46-49).* It all seemed a bit contrived, like the story was planted in the gospels after the fact to fill in the blanks. Like declared earlier, there was no way to know for certain which event was true or untrue after the fact.

    From the age of 12 until he was close to the age of 30 when he was baptized by John the Baptist, Yeshua's life was officially a blank ledger. Perhaps the Passover story was just the scribes of the Universal Church providing some background information on their prophet because they literally had nothing else to offer about this time in his life. But what was most curious was no such event was detailed in the gospel of Matthew where the bulk of the stories of his life were found, from his birth to the beginning of his ministry. Since he was one of the twelve apostles, Matthew was acknowledged to be an eye-witness to many of the accounts he wrote about. Even if he did not witness a particular event, it was likely he knew someone who did. The reasoning was: theoretically Matthew could check on the veracity of the story he was relaying in the gospel.

This Passover story, however, came from the gospel of Luke, a gospel written near the end of the first century of the Common Era. It was written by an individual who did not know Yeshua personally nor any of the people in his life. Ostensibly historians suggested Luke was an associate of the apostle Paul, and accompanied him on his mission. Therefore it must be considered second-hand information and less reliable. While there was no reason to believe the story was fiction, there was no reason to believe it was a true account either. This was not a personal slight against Luke or his intent. Primarily it was an attempt to fill in the blanks on the life of one who meant so much to so many.

For a different reason, the veracity of the story of Yeshua's baptism in the Jordan River was equally suspect. Before Yeshua appeared on the banks of the Jordan River to be baptized by the wilderness prophet John, other than the

Essene and his family members, who knew John was his cousin? It was probable very few knew him or where he came from. *"Then cometh Jesus from Galilee to Jordan unto John, to be baptized of him. But John forbad him saying, I have need to be baptized of thee, and thou comest to me? And Jesus answering said unto him, suffer it to be so now: for thus it becometh us to fulfill all righteousness. Then he suffered him. And Jesus, when he was baptized, went up straightway out of the water: and, lo, the heavens were opened unto him, and he saw the Spirit of God descending like a dove, and lighting upon him; and lo a voice from heaven, saying, 'this is my beloved son, in whom I am well pleased' (Matthew 3: 13-17).*

The story seemed to be suggesting that Yeshua did not know John because he did not acknowledge who he was during the baptism. He certainly did not greet him as a family member would. Perhaps that was because the scribes knew virtually nothing about Yeshua's or John's past in Alexandria. They simply did not know either of them. Furthermore this event occurred before Yeshua collected his disciples so Matthew could not have been present to witness the event. It was probable that the individual who told this story did not know that John was Yeshua's cousin. If he did, John would have been identified as a relative. How did one go from humble peasant carpenter to esteemed Hebrew prophet? Did being baptized in the Jordan River have that effect? That really sounded too absurd to believe anyone would, but the Universal Church was counting on the fact their members would not question it.

It was the contention of the scribes of the Universal Church that Jesus of Nazareth led a quiet, nondescript life as a Hebrew peasant before he began his ministry. That kind of life did not necessarily make one learned, or inclined to embark upon a ministry. Being a carpenter's apprentice would not necessarily mean that he could read or write either. Those skills would not be necessary for his chosen profession. Would this be the kind of upbringing that would suddenly result in him becoming a prophet at thirty years old? That really did not make much sense. If however he was a rabbi, and was being groomed from birth to become one, then it would make sense that he was literate.

In all manner of things, logic should prevail. Unfortunately in matters of Faith was where the authorities of the Universal Church expected their adherents to suspend logic, and just accept whatever they were told whether it made sense or not. Loyalty to the Orthodox brand of

Christianity seemed to overshadow the recognition of real circumstances, or facts for that matter. Logic was never applied to their observance of Faith. In fact, it was discouraged, then and now, by the powers-that-be, and that was the way they liked it. What made sense 2000 years ago was very likely to make sense now, and the converse was true as well.

On the other hand, it could very well be Yeshua spent the lion's share of his youth in Alexandria being schooled in the ways and philosophies of the Essene. The subject matter of his sermons, particularly his Sermon on the Mount, and circumstances of his interactions with the people were indicative of that. It made perfect sense that his training was of utmost importance for him to ascend to the lofty position of the Teacher of Righteousness. Moreover by all accounting, didn't it take time and effort to produce a Christ? They just didn't appear on Earth from out of the blue, did they? One could fully expect training was necessary, and would be handled by the Essene to fill that position. They had already trained and sent forth almost two dozen Hebrew prophets in days gone by. Undoubtedly Yeshua would be the crowning achievement of that development process.

It seemed what the Universal Church wanted their

followers to believe was that a magical formula was required to create a Christ. That would suggest such a designation was made by the Almighty. The Orthodox Christians suggested men had no part in it. That would imply a special type of DNA was involved of the supernatural variety. No Orthodox Christian would ever dispute those findings. In fact, they would quickly point out that Scripture was full of instances that supported their contention that Yeshua was the Son of God who God sent to die for the sins of mankind. The Orthodox would claim it was his mission and his mission alone.

In the canonical gospels, however, Yeshua was fond of saying that others could achieve what he had. On one occasion he said," *Verily, Verily, I say unto you, he that believeth in me, the works that I do shall he do also. And greater works than these shall he do because I go unto my Father. And whatsoever ye shall ask in my name, that I will do, that the Father may be glorified in the Son. If ye shall ask anything in my name, I will do it"* (John 14: 12-14). This statement indicated Yeshua knew that Christhood was a path, and an attainable goal, given one received the right training, put in the effort, and essentially succeeded in their objective. The Essene and the CHILDREN OF THE LAW OF ONE believed the same. The implication was Yeshua knew the process he had gone through, and it was available to others if they met the qualifications. If he did not believe this, the preceding statement would not have been made. The apostle John was merely repeating what it took to be considered God's Logos as Yeshua was, and what steps needed to be undertaken to achieve that status. What Yeshua was actually saying was that one could become the son or daughter of God given the right circumstances.

Therefore Yeshua knew that Christhood was a status one evolved into, rather than being born into. It was very unlikely that could have happened if Jesus had spent his boyhood years in Nazareth training to be a carpenter. The canonical gospels recorded that Jesus of Nazareth exhibited talents and abilities such as healing the sick, performing miracles, reading and writing Scripture, interpreting the Law of Moses, and preaching the Word. Moreover he had an innate understanding of the philosophy of the Word. Furthermore he had the key qualification, being a person of impeccable moral character with a compassionate nature. These were precisely the talents and abilities in which the Essene specialized in instilling in their students. They had a long history of doing precisely that.

The evidence presented indicated Yeshua was a product of his training in the Essene school. That training made him who he became later in life. There was a logical reason for it. It was not the result of a baptism or a magical transformation from illiterate carpenter to esteemed prophet like the scribes of the Universal Church wanted their followers to believe. There was no alchemical transformation involved in the process. There was a logical reason why Yeshua became the Christ. That made more sense than any reason the Orthodox offered, justifying the son of God designation. That designation simply put the achievement out of reach of the simple folk to accomplish as if that was the intent. It did not take a leap of Faith to grasp the meaning of something when there was a logical reason for it. All it took was the comprehension that there was a reason for what one believed; that in and of itself took much of the mystery out of the Christhood of Yeshua as it should.

Chapter 7 The Essene

In 1947 the manuscripts found at Wadi Qumran in caves in the Judean desert adjacent to the Dead Sea, called THE DEAD SEA SCROLLS, revealed a secret society founded upon the principles of Love, Compassion, and Oneness with the Creator. A Brotherhood-Sisterhood of holy men and women, living together in a community, carried within that group the seeds of Christianity and set a course for the future of Western Civilization. From this community emerged individuals who would change the face of the world and alter the course of history. Reportedly several of the principal founders of esoteric Christianity were Essene: Anna and Zachariah, Joseph and Mary, John the Baptist, Yeshua, Mary Magdalene, John the Divine, and the apostles James and Jude. There were no facts in evidence that proved these individuals were Essene. It was simply that most of them were from same family, and supposedly their belief systems appeared to reflect the Essene teachings. Therefore quid proquo made the case the historical record could not. But such was the tenor and landscape of legend and mythology.

Although of Jewish origin, the Essene of Alexandria was a branch of the tribe that had separated itself from

Judea. The speculation was that the Essene was the lost thirteenth tribe of the Israelites, and the reason they were considered lost was because Jewish history had lost track of them. It seemed however they had set themselves apart from the other twelve tribes. Because of the illumination of their inner life and their knowledge of the hidden mysteries of Nature unknown to the remainder of the tribes, some of the Essene also led a separate life in the Judean desert near Wadi Qumran. The discoveries of scrolls in the caves along the Dead Sea were proof the Essene existed, as were Philo's accounts of their lives in Alexandria. The Essene believed that they were Yahweh's sons and daughters of old, and heirs to a great ancient civilization. They possessed their advanced knowledge and worked diligently in secret for the triumph of the light over the darkness of the human mind. The symbolism of Plato's cave and the emergence from it fit neatly within the Essene frame of mind.

In this sense, the Essene was representative of the Great White Brotherhood whose expressed purpose throughout the ages was to keep that light alive in the minds and hearts of humanity. Thus this segment of the Great White Brotherhood felt it had been entrusted with a mission. That mission was to transform humanity by awakening the light in each human being it encountered. As it unfolded, that mission was the establishment of the children of the light as the cornerstone of Western Civilization. It was alleged they were supported in this effort by highly-evolved beings who directed them. These beings were the angelic host, master of wisdom, and hierophants of the ancient arts of mastery of self. It was contended that the Essene knew how to communicate with angelic beings, and had solved the dilemma of the origin of evil on Earth. From this tradition, Yeshua emerged to conquer the world with love, peace, and brotherhood or so his Essene legacy pre-supposed.

The unique philosophy of the Essene was not limited to a single religion, but extracted from each of them their essential principles. It might be said the Essene faith was a Source faith; meaning it was source material from which other religions arose. The Essene considered religion to be a stage in humanity's pre-awakening to the Light, and the knowledge was embodied in the aphorism: All was One. Religion was a stepping stone on the path to the Light. The Essene accorded great importance to the teachings of the ancient Chaldeans, Zoroaster, Hermes Trismegistus (who the Egyptians called Thoth), the secret instructions of Moses, as well as the revelations of Enoch. Their purpose was the perfection of the Christ Consciousness in every human being through the pursuance of Oneness with all Creation. It was enabled by practicing love, brotherhood, and compassion to all they encountered in their daily lives. In their view, a strict adherence to Virtue was the way, rather than Evangelism. One proved through their works the worth of their teachings. They truly believed actions spoke louder than words.

    The Essene regarded themselves as the guardians of the Divine Teaching. They had in their possession many very ancient manuscripts; among them: the books of the Jewish prophets, The Torah Moses had written, the Talmud, the **BOOK OF JUBILEES** (the original Creation myth), and the five books of Enoch as well as their communal literature. In the school of the Essene, students spent their time decoding manuscripts, translating, and reproducing them to perpetuate and preserve the esoteric knowledge they contained. In the monastery style of life they preferred, it was work they deemed sacred. The Essene considered their Brotherhood-Sisterhood as the presence on Earth of the teachings of the sons and daughters of the Light. In their communal literature, there were abundant references to the children of the light and the children of the darkness. The Essene believed that they embodied the Light which shone in the darkness, inviting the darkness to transform itself into Light, or flee before it. By all accounts, a living faith, like the Essene possessed, would be proven superior to any ideology contrived to coerce compliance to Universal Law.

In Jerusalem, there was even a door that bore their name: the Door of the Essene. One who walked through that door was said to become whole because those that lived behind it were well-versed in the teachings of the angelic host. They welcomed the sincere seeker into their midst: man, woman, or child. Thus for the Essene, when a candidate for the school asked to be admitted, it meant that within that person, the process of the awakening of the soul was set in motion. Such a soul was ready to climb the stairs of the sacred temple of humanity. In other words, ascend to that station and be one with the sons and daughters of Yahweh.

In their teachings, the Essene differentiated between

the souls that were sleeping, drowsy, and awakened. Their task was to help, to comfort, and to relieve the sleeping souls, to try to awaken the drowsy souls, and to welcome and guide the awakened souls. Only the souls considered to be awakened could be initiated into the mysteries of the Brotherhood-Sisterhood. For the candidate, it began a path of evolution that would take him or her out of the cycle of their incarnations. Once one exited the Wheel of Life, one ventured down the path to Christ Consciousness. All other steps taken were away from that goal.

The Hebrews of the other twelve tribes knew of the Essene. From this lineage and school, the greatest Hebrew prophets came to instruct the other tribes in the ways of the Spirit. The prophets were both feared and respected for their knowledge and power. To the prophets of Israel, Yahweh was a supreme being who created Man in ITS own image. Hence to IT was assigned superhuman qualities. Yahweh was considered to be the Creator of all worlds, physical and spiritual, of which IT was the lord and overseer. Thus they reasoned IT was personally involved with every aspect of Creation and subsequently every creeping thing upon the Earth, including the human being. Because of the special status accorded the human being as the crown of creation,

Yahweh enacted laws to assist ITS chosen species on how-to live-in accordance with ITS design. These Seven Laws of Creation were represented by angelic beings who administered them: Order, Balance, Harmony, Growth, God-Perception, Love, and Compassion. Through spiritual expression of these Principles acting upon matter, those souls on the path were guided to completion.

The prophets of Israel carried it one step further by declaring the Israelites were Yahweh's chosen people, and as such shouldered a burden other ethnic groups did not share. They were the recipients of Yahweh's favor because it was, they who had made a covenant with Yahweh by receiving ITS laws through Moses in the form of the Ten Commandments. They claimed not only did Yahweh appear to Moses in the form of a burning bush on Mount Sinai, but with a fiery finger burned the essence of ITS code of ethics into two stone tablets for posterity. Such an act emphasized the serious nature of this transference of celestial wisdom, and underscored a belief that they were indeed destined to receive it. A vessel was fashioned to carry the tablets. It was called the Ark of the Covenant.

Specifically the role of the Hebrew prophets was to be Yahweh's human representatives on Earth, in principle and practice. Ostensibly their role was to ensure the Hebrew race continued to be worthy of Yahweh's favor, and live as the Deity would live if IT were a human being. The entire focus of the prophets' existence on Earth was to notify the people when they had strayed from the narrow path of righteousness. The prophets were the Conscience of the chosen people, never letting them forget what was owed and to whom. Emerging from the deserts of the Judean wilderness, when necessary, from their Essene sanctuary, they pointed the way to selfless service and strict obedience of Yahweh's directives. Furthermore they knew full well what Yahweh had ordained because they were the keepers of that covenant.

    To the scribes of the Essene had been attributed the writing of the books of the Old Testament prophets. At the very least they were responsible for preserving the Torah and Talmud, original fragments of which were found in the caves of Qumran in present-day Jordan. Known as THE DEAD SEA SCROLLS, they symbolized the conscience and memory of the Israelites, both historical and apocryphal. With vim and vigor the prophets assumed the mantle of faith and never allowed the people to waver from their holy commitment. The prophets reasoned: that if Yahweh were to come down from on high to establish the covenant, it must mean it was incumbent upon them not to shirk their responsibility in upholding their end. These beliefs laid the foundation of the Judeo-Christian expression of faith as it existed today.

The Egyptians knew of the Essene as well. They referred to them as the healers and the doctors. They had property in Alexandria and the community as a whole felt respect and esteem for the Essene because of their honesty, pacifism, goodness, discretion, and their talent as healers. That talent was devoted to the poorest as well as the richest. The healings they performed were of the mind, body, and spirit, whatever was required for wholeness. Selfless service required no payment. The payment was that it be returned in kind. Their kindness was paid forward for all time.

Moreover even if the Brotherhood-Sisterhood was very strict about the law of secrecy with regard to its internal doctrine, it cultivated many points of contact with the people in general. That was through places of lodging for the pilgrims from every horizon, through helpful actions in difficult periods, and especially through the healing of illnesses. These places of primary teaching and of healing were located in precise areas where people go freely.

A unique teaching of the Essene was the recognition

of the equality of the sexes. With all due respect, they accorded to women the place which was rightfully theirs. Thus women were able to participate in all of the spiritual activities. The Essene offered an esoteric teaching on androgyny which provided them with a perception of the soul beyond the dualistic conception of sex. The white linen robe which was issued to all members of the group was a symbol of this vision of the soul's unity. As members of the Great White Brotherhood, the brothers and sisters of the Essene tribe were robed in white. Their life-in-spirit was devoid of the concerns of gender, egoism, and materialism, as the kingdom of Yahweh should always be. The community being neither matriarchal nor patriarchal in character, their union sought equality, fraternity, and Justice for all.

The typical daily life of the Essene depended upon where the members lived. There were those who lived in the villages surrounded by a low wall, completely cut-off from the cities, in the middle of nature. Their life was simple, austere, and pious, lulled into a rhythm by the seasons, by the days of celebration, and by visitors. Other lived in the cities like Alexandria, in large buildings which belonged to the Community, and which served simultaneously as their home, as an inn, and as a hospital. The Essene devoted their time to healing the sick, and to providing hospitality to strangers passing through. There were others who traveled the roads, circulating news, and information around all of their centers spread out in every country.

The Essene strongly condemned slavery and all forms of servility. No Essene was allowed to have a servant. That was considered a sin; as was working only to make money which, in their estimation, translated into another kind of slavery. Slavery and servility were, for them, things related to the existence of dark and demonic entities, and belonged to what they called, *the world of divine anger*. According to their communal literature, the Essene was on Earth to combat darkness with love and compassion. Once the ego was set aside, the Essene taught that peace and harmony would once again reign on Earth. Hence it could be inferred the Essene clung to a notion that a Golden Age of peace and harmony once existed on Earth, from which humanity had fallen from into its present state. One could call that place Eden which will be further discussed when the text shifted to a discussion of THE CHILDREN OF THE LAW OF ONE in a later chapter.

Any man or woman who was even remotely affiliated with the community had to free his or her slaves and abstain from eating meat. For the Essene, slavery was also tied to the fact of being carnivorous, because the ones, who could not stop eating animal flesh and drinking blood, could not control the passions of an animalistic nature. Therefore one could not think in a clear manner. One was reduced to slavery by his or her nature. Selfishness was forsaken in the offering of selfless service to any who required it. Selflessness was an attribute Yeshua acquired in his association with the group, and he carried it with him the remainder of his life.

It was the Essene who taught Yeshua, the Teacher of Righteousness, to eat, to walk, to speak, to read, to write, to pray, and to heal by uniting himself with the One With No Name (Yahweh), and with the Father and the Mother forces of the world, the everlasting eternal Trinity. When Yeshua went out into the world, he benefited from having a purpose provided by the Essene. For all intents and purposes, their mission was interrupted historically at Masada during the Jewish tax rebellion of 66 CE. However Yeshua's mission carried on in one form or another to this very day. In both cases, it proved to be the Roman Empire that stood in the way of its realization. In this sense, *the world of divine anger* represented by the empire won that battle, but the war of the light versus the darkness raged on as the Book of Revelation contended.

In a historical sense, the Gnostics attempted to pick up where the Essene left off, taking up the cause of the Essene and moving it forward. What they did not factor in was that Orthodox Christianity would not cooperate with the Essene mission. It had a mission of its own: that was to spread its doctrine across the face of the Earth with missionary zeal. Unfortunately the mission of Orthodox Christianity was developed and executed in league with *the world of divine anger*. Thus the mission was corrupted by its needs and desires under the auspices of the Holy Roman Empire. To this day, its ways and means held sway over every aspect of human existence in some form or another.

In essence Orthodox Evangelism served the cause of the empire, the missionary arm of a Holy Roman Empire which was established by the forces of Orthodox Christianity and the might of the Roman Empire to conquer the hearts and minds of the human race. It's way was: God's will be done, foisting a brand of religious colonialism upon an unsuspecting populace. That was not the Essene way which in many cases was the way of liberty, democracy and free will. It was for individuals to enlist in the mission of their own accord. The way of the Essene and the mantle of the Great White Brotherhood were carried on by THE CHILDREN OF THE LAW OF ONE when that group migrated to Tibet. That transition will be described in more detail in a subsequent chapter. As always who was right and who was wrong was often determined by the one left standing after the dust cleared in a historical sense, and remembrance often hung in the balance.

Chapter 8 The Nag Hammadi Library

In 1945 the first of certain Gnostic documents were unearthed in Egypt. In total they were called THE NAG HAMMADI LIBRARY. They were found in stone jars hidden in caves near the modern city of Nag Hammadi along the banks of the Nile River. A group of Stanford scholars and international researchers led by James M. Robinson translated and studied the texts. Their study was first published in 1977 in an anthology, entitled, THE NAG HAMMADI LIBRARY. This book launched the modern study of the Gnostic movement.

It exposed a phenomenon during the infancy of Christianity, revealing the overall Christian movement to be heterogeneous rather than homogeneous in nature. The material of the library spanned the pantheistic heritage of religious thought from Egypt, Greece, India, and Persia and combined it with the teachings of the Christ. Cults with leanings toward Neo-Platonism, Hermeticism, and Zorasterism figured prominently in the dialogues. Individual codices were written to suggest Yeshua was well-versed in these philosophies and referenced them in his teachings. The writers of these documents were the forbearers of the Coptic Christian movement that sprang up in Egypt and

Syria in the first century of the Common Era.

    The operative question would be: was it Yeshua who blended philosophies in his teachings or the writers of the documents? It also begged the question of how and why the documents in question came to be in those mason jars. This manuscript was not a study of those documents per se but of the people who wrote them. Their brief history of a few hundred years could be compared to a meteor streaking through the sky. It was seen for a moment in time and then dissipated. What was notable about their sundry philosophies was the attempt to link them to contemporary pagan mystery schools whether they were Persian, Greek, Egyptian, or Roman. It seemed to the writers of the documents in question, it was necessary to provide continuity for the human religious experience. That experience was a renewal connecting with the teachings of the Christ, evidencing a new globalist approach to the philosophy. It pointed out the fact that when human beings were confronted with a new expression, they attempted to draw comparisons with old expressions. In some cases, a blend of the old and the new was attempted. It was only human nature to make these comparisons. Building bridges to the past was a distinctly human activity, and it was generally undertaken for the sake of continuity. In this case, it would be a continuity of religious experience. However whether or not it was appropriate to include Christianity in that continuity of experience was a matter of spirited debate then and now.

Since the initial discovery of the texts in 1945 and in the years that followed, the divine right of spiritual authority claimed by the Church of Rome was called into question. When one considered how the Church received its right of inheritance, by social and political manipulation, persecution of its enemies, and the enslavement of innocent heathen populations through missionary evangelism, one could not deny the influence of manifest destiny. Also it became apparent that the objective of ideological purity and uniformity within the dogma of the rank and file of the Universal Church was achieved at the expense of human life, liberty, and the pursuit of happiness. In this case, happiness would equate to worshipping one's God in the manner of one's choosing, rather than have it dictated to them.

The history of the Universal Church, or Catholicism, showed its actions to be inconsistent and contradictory with the methods and practices of the man, known as the Christ. Henceforth it could not be a product of his life, mission, or philosophical expression. If alive today, the expectation was that Yeshua would flatly deny the legitimacy of the reign of the Universal Church, and his designation as its founder. Once he caught a glimpse of the majesty and splendor of The Roman Catholic Church and opulence which it flaunted, he would even refuse participation if his reaction could be projected from his historical words and deeds. Yeshua would have responded the same as he did when he cast the moneychangers out of the temple in Jerusalem; for the moneychangers were one and the same, Christian, pagan, or Jew. *"And when he was come into Jerusalem, all the city was moved, saying, who is this? And the multitude said 'this is Jesus the prophet of Nazareth of Galilee'. And Jesus went into the temple of God, cast out all of them that sold and bought in the temple, and overthrew the tables of the moneychangers, and the seats of them that sold doves. And he said unto them, it is written, my house shall be called the house of prayer; but ye have made it a den of thieves"* (Matthew 21: 10-13).

Unfortunately for the masses, the Church Fathers felt little or no shame. The infestation of mammon into the bowels of the Church persisted to this very day, and it perverted all that it touched. One thing was for certain; thoroughly mythologizing the personage of Yeshua enhanced the position of the Universal Church, rather than detracted from it. When it came to Evangelism, the motivation to tell a tale to make its case more appealing became obvious. The operative question would be: was it Yeshua who espoused Church philosophy or the evangelists who spoke for him? Given the answer the follow-up question became: to whom did Christianity belong? Some experts in the study of Theology have said Saul of Tarsus, who took the name Paul, the greatest evangelist of all time, was the founder of the Universal Church. However it would be unfair that he should shoulder all the blame for an experiment gone awry. He did not coerce anyone into the faith, nor derived personal gain from it, unless one considered fame a personal gain. The first and greatest evangelist was a homeless man unlike his many successors who excelled at passing the collection plate and amassing fortunes. It just happened he presented the most effective and appealing arguments for belief in the teachings of Yeshua the Christ.

It was important to note at this time that Paul only knew the Christ by reputation unlike the twelve apostles who knew the man. The incident *On the road to Damascus* (ACTS OF THE APOSTLES, 9) when Paul saw the apparition of the Christ that knocked him off his horse, it constituted the main focus of his contact with the Christ. His turnabout from being a persecutor of Christians to the premier follower of Christ was equally stunning. According to the Scriptures, Saul was blinded by the Light. Once he converted to the Light, then Paul could see. The process of conversion to Christianity was not so dramatic for most that went through the process, but Paul was deemed a special case. He was a walking, talking billboard of missionary zeal, the first of its kind, created by a paranormal version of The Pentecost. Therefore there was a distinct difference from the experience of the other apostles.

However Paul's views were accepted by the Gentiles because he put them into an understandable human framework. He could not have foreseen his views of Christian philosophy could become so perverted by the materialistic goals of his ideological progeny. The width and breadth of this perversion was forecasted in the book of REVELATION but few recognized it as such. In real terms, it revealed the inherent danger of missionary zeal gone awry. For that reason, an expose of the history of Christianity was in order. Perhaps it would put the matter into the proper perspective.

Before delving into the topic of Gnostic Christianity, one must consider its origins. Ostensibly it sprang from the lips of Yeshua. But where did the Gnostics get their knowledge? What were the origins? Was it possible they made it all up or did they borrow from older traditions? The case was made in a previous chapter in the text that Yeshua was a product of the Essene tribe like every other Hebrew prophet. That only made sense. Some of the Gnostic sects took their lead from the Essene tribe, especially in Alexandria. It was probable that after Masada fell the Essene in Alexandria blended together with the Gnostics rather than the other twelve Jewish tribes. They could have done that for survival or they found something in the Gnostic way that appealed to them. Of course that was only speculation because the trail had gone cold. No one could say with certainty what happened to the Essene.

Philo of Alexandria was also claimed by the Alexandrian Gnostics as a forbearer of their doctrine. Therefore it was appropriate, he was mentioned here. He provided a link in the philosophical tradition between Gnostic Christianity and the Essene, Neo-Platonism, and the Law of Moses. Until the NAG HAMMADI LIBRARY was discovered no one had any clue the Judeo-Christian philosophy had a legitimate connection with Gnosticism, and that any links could be drawn between them. Perhaps one could say with confidence all that had changed now.

Chapter 9 The Descent To Untruth

Christianity came into being in a violent age; the result of a crucifixion at Golgotha, a resurrection from the dead three days later, and the diverse interpretations of those events that ensued thereafter. From the beginning, the diversity of opinion created by the acts of the Christ, particularly the resurrection, spawned a multitude of expressions. As soon as Christians began to practice their creed, they began to disagree as to how it should be practiced. The variety of opinions led to the formation of various Christianized sects which operated within a network of Christian communities in a free enterprise array. That arrangement persisted until the balance of power was tipped in favor of the Roman Christians in the 4th Century of the Common Era.

The discoveries of the DEAD SEA SCROLLS at Wadi Qumran in Jordan, and the NAG HAMMADI LIBRARY in Nag Hammadi, Egypt reinforced the supposition of religious turmoil. In some of the Gnostic gospels found in Nag Hammadi, selected passages from the canonical gospels of Matthew, Mark, Luke, and John were contained. Others showed evidence of Neo-Platonic, pagan, and hermetic influences on the Christian faith. Still others like the Gospel of Mary or Pistis Sophia centered on the role of women in the Christian faith. One woman in particular was showcased. It was Mary Magdalene who many Gnostics claimed was the consort of the Savior, and his second-in-command rather than the widely-accepted notion of it being, the apostle, Simon Peter. One logical reason to believe that Mary Magdalene was considered the second-in-command was the Essene notion of the inherent equality of men and women. Since it appeared to be logical that the Christ was a member of that tribe, those beliefs carried forward to the Gnostics. However to say there was a wide variety of philosophical influences would be an understatement of the highest order. The Gnostic faith was a veritable smorgasbord of Christian offerings in the first four centuries of the Common Era.

    The Gnostic gospels chronicled the emergence of Coptic Christianity, and the early years of turbulence within the global Christian community. They identified the Palestinian Christianity of James the Just, founder of the Jerusalem Church, as the root of several Christian sects which surfaced to claim a share of Christianity. It was followed by the appearance of the Alexandrian (Egyptian), Syrian, Greek, Persian, and Roman brands. Each of these brands claimed a lineage from one or more of the apostles.

Other brands claimed a lineage from a teacher who did not have a direct lineage from Yeshua, but was labeled an esteemed and learned colleague. This of course was a determination made on the substance of the teaching by the adherents of the teacher. Some were mentioned in the biblical book, THE ACTS OF THE APOSTLES, like the followers of Simon Magus and the Manicheans. These were clearly identified as heretics primarily because they were considered to be competitors of the apostles by Orthodox Christians.

By the end of the 4th century of the Common Era, all of these sects except one, the Christian sect founded in Rome, were declared to be heresy by the Roman Catholic authority and officially banned. The Catholic treatment of history has clouded the issue regarding who the heretics actually were and the reasons for their heresy. That could be because the Universal Church had a vested interest in concealing the motives of the heretics as well as its own interest in suppressing them. Several chapters that follow detail the content and disposition of the various heresies. These details were offered to reinforce the notion that all Christians were not in agreement on the content of Christian doctrine.

At the heart of the controversy was the issue of the

rightness or wrongness of the actions of the Universal Church against the heretics given the historical evidence. This was separate from the perceived rightness or wrongness of the particular doctrine in question. It was an issue of earthly dominion, and who had the right to possess it. Truly what made one set of doctrine more valid than another, or was it simply a case of might makes right?

Chapter 10 The Issue Of Gnosis

Before Roman Catholicism asserted itself, two prevailing schools of Christian thought, Gnostic and Orthodox, vied for doctrinal supremacy. These two distinct versions of Christianity respectively opposed each other in content, method, and expression. Though both derived their esoteric principles from the teaching of the Christ, they clashed in the application of those principles, drawing different conclusions and growing in different directions. While the Orthodox broadcasted an exoteric doctrine designed for mass consumption through a missionary mandate, the Gnostics practiced their rituals of self-realization privately in small groups. Both were essentially Christian but their different perspectives produced dissimilar philosophies and practices. Typically the Gnostic approach was more inner-directed, while the Orthodox one was more outer-directed.

In the Orthodox scheme of faith, rote practice and allegiance to leagues of bishops and deacons was stressed, rather than the Gnostic emphasis upon an understanding of the relationship of God and Man. The Orthodox devised theological disciplines to maintain a status quo within the hierarchy of the Universal Church, and in the interpretation and practice of the Word. Their faith was hardened along traditional lines and accepted sources of information. No provision was provided for variances in interpretation based upon personal experience or intuitive insight. It was a first step taken in the process of standardizing the practice of Christian faith, moving toward institutionalization.

As Orthodox doctrine became more rigid and formalized, Gnostic principle evolved in the opposite direction. The Gnostic faith offered its adherents the alternative of Gnosis which was loosely defined as a process of attaining knowledge through contemplative means. Gnosis, a Greek word loosely translated as knowledge, was identified as with that intangible quality of self that was activated by the acceptance of Truth, and devotion to pure Thought. Through the process, the knowledge gained was a realization of the Divine Self, and its relationship to the Creative Force that spawned it. In theory, the process of Gnosis was identified with an initiation into the pagan Mysteries, reminiscent of the spiritual formula used by the ancient Tibetans, Hindus, Egyptians, and Essene with Christian overtones added.

Although essentially Christian in content, Gnosticism reached far beyond the diluted dogma of the

Universal Church, it made a conscious effort to connect Christian faith with the ancient mystery schools. In the first few centuries of the Common Era, Gnostic teachers such as Simon Magus, Basilides and Origen of Alexandria, formulated a version of Christian mysticism. To make it viable, Gnostic mysticism incorporated spiritual concepts from the ancient mystery schools of Egypt, Greece, India, and Tibet. These concepts included: the Mother/Father concept of God, the Father/Mother/Son form of Trinity, the Creative Life of the Soul, pantheism, reincarnation, and the role of women in Christianity. In particular, reincarnation was a prominent feature of the Hindu and Tibetan mystery religions.

Though small in numbers, relatively speaking, the Gnostics were strong in spirit with a faith that was qualitative as opposed to the commercialized, quantitative version of Orthodox Christianity. The ceremonial blandishments of Orthodox dogma sharply contrasted the experience of self proposed by Gnosis. While the Gnostics spoke of reunification with the Pleroma (All), the Orthodox clamored for the unification of the Universal Church. In that effort, they erected shrines to rally believers and fashioned relics like crosses and chalices to signify a bond of indulgence. The Gnostics saw folly in idol worship and shunned the Orthodox houses of worship, preferring instead the quietude of Natural surroundings. The appreciation for the beauty of Nature and respect for Natural Law ultimately translated into a reverence for all life. Few of the Orthodox persuasion realized it because it was not a Christian prerogative to see God as Nature, and Nature as God. That prerogative was narrowed to human affairs; i.e., *do unto others as you would have them do unto you.* As for the Orthodox Christians, the ethics of human behavior was never extended as far as applying that moral code to all living things.

    Simon Magus who was credited historically with the founding of the Syrian branch of Gnosticism, was a magician and philosopher mentioned prominently in the New Testament, THE ACTS OF THE APOSTLES, as an adversary of Peter. Simon Magus inspired hate and fear from Orthodox Christians who observed his miracles and declared they were the work of the devil. He, however, was much more than a mere conjuror of natural forces or one who mesmerizes the populace with his tricks as he was described in the New Testament. His philosophical renderings in the first Century of the Common Era set the tone for 300 years of Gnostic thought. The principles of Gnosticism were aptly expressed in a statement preserved by the scholar and historian Hippolytus, called *The Origin of the World*.

> *To you, therefore, I say what I say, and write what I write. And it writing is this: of its universal Aeons, periods, planes, or cycles of creative and created life in substance and space, [and] celestial creatures, there are two shoots, without beginning or end, springing from one Root which is the power indivisible, inapprehensible silence, Bythos. Of these shoots one is manifested from above, which is the Great Power, the Universal Mind ordering all things male, and it other [is manifested] from below, the Great Thought, female producing all things. hence pairing with each other, they unite and manifest the Middle Distance, Incomprehensible Air, without beginning or end. In this is the Father who sustains all things, and nourishes those things which have a beginning and end.*

This statement expressed the Gnostic view of Creation which was reiterated countless times in the writings of those Gnostics that followed. Not only was it issued from the Simonian sect that Simon Magus formed, but from the Syrian cult as a whole; for it tended to follow his conceptual lead. His Creation history could be capsulated as follows: manifestation was the result of reacting positive and negative principles which interacted within a middle plane or point equilibrium called the Pleroma. It was an ethereal substance produced from the intermingling of spiritual and material universes. From the Pleroma was individualized the Demiurges (analogous to the Hebrew Jehovah) which was the lord of physical creation. His cosmic counterpart, the Pistis Sophia (Wisdom), provided the animation necessary to give matter, life. It was described by Simon in his work, PHILOSOPHUMENIA, as three pairs of opposites called Syzygies emanated from the Eternal One. The six living Divine principles or Aeons listed in the order of their creation were: first, Mind (Nous) and Thought (Epinoia), second, Voice (Phone) and Name (Onoma), and third, Reason (Logismos) and Reflection (Enthumesis). When these six Aeons interacted in unison, as in a cause-and-effect chain-reaction, all forms of action ensued. According to the wisdom of Simon, the Christ was the embodiment of the first Syzygy, Nous, and through him were expressed the totality of these divine principles. It thus served as the primary example of the divine man, or perfect human being.

An Alexandrian philosopher, Basilides, claiming initiation from the apostle Matthew, postulated metaphysical theories combining Egyptian hermeticism, Oriental Occultism, Chaldean Astrology, and Persian philosophy into a single expression. That hybrid expression within mixed with Christian mysticism produced a variety of Gnostic strains. Many of them were represented in the cache of manuscripts from the NAG HAMMADI LIBRARY. To Basilides was attributed the conception of Abraxas, the God of good and evil, and Pantheos which was the belief that God was the sum of the All. The All was divided into 365 Aeons that when added to each other comprised the Supreme Being. Because of his Neo-Platonic leanings, Basilides attempted to unify the pagan mysteries with the emerging schools of Christianity. In his sphere of influence, Alexandria, Egypt, his philosophy flourished.

To Basilides was also attributed the founding of the Catechetical School of Alexandria, Egypt. It was established circa 180 CE as one of the great centers of Christian scholarship. It was instituted to bridge the gap between Classical and Christian education. The intent was to revitalize an intellectual community with the pre-Christian wisdom of Greece and Egypt; for the achievements of Science and Mysticism respectively were prized by its founders. It boasted the esoteric wisdom of the Egyptian Mystery schools of Isis and Osiris, and the Greek Academy of Plato. From it were graduated a series of brilliant intellects like Origen and Clement who were able to integrate the long-standing pagan Science and Philosophy with the emerging Christian Philosophy.

Philo of Alexandria, an ex-patriot Jew, and consummate historian and philosopher, was credited with laying the groundwork for the school. Though it was founded many years after he passed away, his work in the shadow and substance of the Library at Alexandria laid a foundation connecting Classical Greek, Jewish, and Christian scholarship. Among his accomplishments was compiling a historical record of the Essene. Little of his work survived to this day, but reportedly it concurred with the DEAD SEA SCROLLS found in desert of Judea in 1945. Clement and Origen, both of Alexandria, were credited with providing a continuing philosophical basis for the school, and making it a force in the developing Christian world. Both of these men profoundly influenced Christian thought of their day, and were revered in the Alexandrian community as leading figures of early Christianity in Egypt.

As for the Nag Hammadi manuscripts, they represented the Scripture upon which the Coptic Christian Church was founded in Alexandria. Many of the Nag Hammadi codices were written in Greek, and then translated to Coptic. They were traced back to this time period circa 200 CE. They were probably the work of teachers and students of the Catechetical School. Being so moved by their exposure to esoteric Christianity, their words were committed to papyrus, copper, and leather. Typically their work was apocalyptic in tone, and introduced a variety of intellectual and spiritual topics at variance with Orthodox ideology. But some texts revealed a preoccupation with pre-historical events, such as the origin of the world. It indicated a record was being kept for historical as well as religious reasons. The Gnostics wrote as voluminously as their Orthodox counterparts, but the former's works remained largely unknown due to the circumstances of their demise. However Orthodox literature survived to this day partly because the Universal Church was so successful in suppressing the Gnostic versions.

Not all Gnostics were necessarily Christian as it would be strictly defined. It would be more appropriate to define them as Jewish-Christian, neo-platonic-Christian, or pantheistic-Christian because particular brands were hybrid versions of Christianity. The reason for these distinctions was that various sects retained previous beliefs from their pre-Christian lives.

An example of this transition from an initiation into the Pagan Mysteries to baptism in the Christian faith was aptly expressed in the Gnostic text, *The Vision of Poimandres*. In this text, the writer, a hermetic philosopher, addressed his prayer for guidance to Thoth Hermes. Typically it represented a similar oath that one would express to their savior, Jesus and God the Father if they would be Orthodox Christian.

> "Blessed art thou, O Son of Light, to whom of all men, I, Poimandres, the Light of the World, have revealed myself. I order you to go forth, to become as a guide to those who wander in darkness, that all men within who dwells the spirit of My Mind [The Universal Mind] may be saved by My Mind within you, which shall call forth My Mind in them. Establish My Mysteries and they shall not fail from its Earth, for I am the Mind of The Mysteries and until Mind fails (which is never) my Mysteries cannot fail". With these parting words, Poimandres, radiant with celestial light, vanished, mingling with the powers of the heavens. Raising his eyes unto the heavens, Hermes blessed the Father of ALL THINGS and consecrated his life to the service of the Great Light. Thus preached Hermes: "O people of the earth, men Born and made of the elements, but with the spirit of The Divine Man within you, rise from your sleep of ignorance! Be sober and thoughtful. Realize that your home is not in the earth but in the Light. Why have you delivered yourselves over unto death, having the power to partake of immortality? Repent, and change your minds. Depart from the dark light and forsake corruption forever. Prepare your selves to climb through the Seven Rings and to blend your souls with the eternal Light.

In so much as the previous oath of allegiance offered a

plea for knowledge and guidance, the conclusion of this text revealed the answer returned. As one was initiated into the pagan Mysteries as well as the Christian faith by the same motto "*ask and ye shall receive*". In both cases the initiates asked for Gnosis. The difference between them in the Word received was: Reason versus Faith. For the pagan initiate, knowledge was a function of reason. While for the Christian initiate, knowledge was a function of faith. The aim of the Gnostic teachers was to merge the two into one expression.

> *The sleep of the body is the sober watchfulness of the mind and the shutting of my eyes reveal the true Light. My silence is filled with budding life and hope, and is full of good. My words are the blossoms of fruit from the tree of my soul. For this is the faithful account of what I received from my true Mind, that is Poimandres, the Great Dragon, the Lord of the Word, through which I became inspired by God with the Truth. Since that day my Mind has been ever with me and in my soul it hath given birth to the Word: thy Word is Reason, and Reason hath redeemed me. For which cause, with all of my soul and all my strength, I give praise and blessing unto God the Father, the Life and the Light, and the Eternal Good.*

Since the process of becoming a Christian entailed a conversion, it was likely to have been a slow process by which previous beliefs were not eradicated, but altered instead. Generally gentiles did not become Christianized in an instant. It took some time. While the change was ideally one of behavior modification, it was also ritualistic. Hence the development of the Orthodox Christian and the Gnostic Christian could differ so greatly in thought and deed. It could be construed they did not practice the same faith. Eventually both sides came to this realization. While the whole world knew what became of Orthodox Christianity, few never realized nor sympathized with the fate of the Gnostics.

During the violent persecutions of Roman Emperors, Severus, Decius, Valerian, and Galatian during the 3rd century of the Common Era, Egyptian Gnostics were driven underground for survival. To preserve their faith, it was recorded on papyrus and leather scrolls which chronicled their Christian awareness during trying times. The use of the Coptic language would suggest authorship from or translation by the Egyptian populace. The texts, in general, were Gnostic in ideology meaning there was a common thread of philosophical concurrence in an umbrella type variety of perspective. Not all presented Christian themes, such as those attributed to the followers of Hermes Trismegistus and Zoroaster which would indicate that not all Gnostics were Christian as one would strictly define it. Simonians, Sethians,

Manicheans, and Valentinians, although representing different quarrelsome sects did unite in the face of the common peril, namely the Romans. In fact the Egyptian Gnostics were represented by a council for a time which would indicate that official Gnosticism was a localized phenomenon predominant in Egypt. While Gnostic communities probably did exist in Syria, North Africa, and various locales in Asia Minor, it was likely, however, that Alexandria was the hub of Gnosticism in the first four centuries of the Common Era.

Because Syrian and North African Gnostic communities resembled the Essene community in Wadi Qumran, it has been suggested that some considered themselves to be a continuation of the Essene tradition with a philosophical face-lift. The Essene seemed to have disappeared historically circa 70 CE with the Roman conquest of Judea which effectively crushed a Jewish tax-rebellion. The Gnostic movement in Egypt began to gather momentum and took shape some 50 years later. The large Jewish ex-patriot population in Alexandria provided a fertile breeding ground for these religious hybrids. Notably the classical version of Palestinian Christianity as taught by James the Just, the brother of Yeshua, a genealogy suggested by Gnostic records, was influenced by Essene mysticism extensively and Neo-Platonist ideas to a small degree.

Between Orthodox and Gnostic Christians there were many divergences of opinions on the Christian faith. Propagation of the faith, martyrdom, and the authority of Peter as leader were chief among them. This conflict of purpose weighed heavily upon the minds of the learned men, Orthodox and Gnostic alike. While the infancy of the Christian movement was marked by doctrinal struggles for supremacy, Gnostic sect versus Gnostic sect, or Orthodox sect versus Gnostic sect, there was a conciliatory attitude of grudging acceptance among them, early on. That was because pagan Rome was a constant threat for both Orthodox and Gnostic sects alike. It persisted until the size of the Universal Church dictated a change in policy.

Chapter 11 The Propagation Of The Faith

The Orthodox and Gnostic approaches to Christianity had many points of conflict; chief among them was the method to propagate the Christian faith. As the Orthodox plotted the formation of a Church which could claim universal membership, the Gnostic preferred a life of simplicity and contemplation like the Essene did. The idea of a Universal Church was shared by Orthodox and Gnostic alike but they disagreed as to its composition and focus. The Orthodox saw it as the material body of Christ as it was manifested by humanity, a building housing a congregation. The Gnostics, however, envisioned it to be a church-within fashioned by the individual. Consequently the penitent kneelers of the Orthodox persuasion sharply contrasted the meditative posture of Gnostic prayer. From the Gnostic point of view, Orthodox Christians knelt before the altar of sacrifice; for as the Gnostics would say they had much for which to be penitent. Their faith in practice left much to be desired in the opinion of the Gnostic community, all show and little substance.

It greatly disturbed a majority of Gnostic Christians that the Orthodox churches opened their doors to all without regard for their qualifications, seeking to swell its ranks for political survival. The Gnostic way may have been a carryover from how the pagan mystery schools and Essene operated. For the price of admission to them, one had to prove one's worth. Gnostics contended that the spiritual blueprint that the Christ had proposed for humankind was neglected or ignored by the Orthodox scheme. That blueprint required spiritual aspirants to emulate a life of purity in thought, word, and deed to the best of their ability. The Orthodox use of Baptism to initiate converts to Christian life was declared to be inadequate by the Gnostics because it was only a symbolic representation of purity. At best it was ceremonial lip-service. Gnostics protested against the enrollment of gentiles in the Christian brotherhood without the proper initiation, which in the Gnostic view was unknown to the Orthodox multitudes. Before gentiles understood the esoteric principles of Christianity they were herded into the Christian corral. This, Gnostics contended, was a situation which discredited the sacrifice of the Christ. That sacrifice they claimed was designed to display the actual achievements of the Anointed One who exhibited in his life and works the true meaning of the Creative Life of the Soul. Instead they observed the soul being neglected in the ever-expanding body of the Universal Church. It generated a vast congregation of Christian-gentiles who believed without understanding. In their view, blind faith rendered the Master's sacrifice a vain one.

Hierakas of Leontopolis, Egypt, circa 300 CE to whom was attributed authorship of *The Testimony of Truth*, an Egyptian Gnostic codex, described the actual insincerity of Orthodox Christianity. Though his description specifically referred to the Orthodox Christians of his day, the analogy could be drawn to the orthodox thinker of any era. Because the need to know oneself was universal and timeless, in the absence of knowing, self-delusion existed for all time. Easily the condition could be applied to spiritual aspirants from any era that relied upon Authority to point the way. In the absence of knowledge, the Gnostics contended, every manner of perversion of pure Thought was evident. It resulted in error.

> *The foolish thinking in their [the Orthodox] heart that if they confess, 'we are Christians', in word only [but] not with power, while giving themselves over to Ignorance, to human death; not knowing where they are going nor who Christ is, thinking that they will live, when they are [really] in error, hasten toward it principalities and the Authorities. They fall into their clutches because of the Ignorance that is in them. For [if] only words which*

bear testimony were affecting salvation, the whole world would endure this thing and would be saved. But in this way, they drew error to themselves. From its inception the purpose of Orthodox indoctrination had been aimed at stilling the inquiring mind, and in stalling in its place an unquestioned certainty carved in stone. Clearly the legacy of Orthodox indoctrination was full of examples showing that the Orthodox viewed their position as unassailable. At this juncture, it was not necessary to recount the theological tale of woe in all of its glory. If one could not accept that declaration for what it was, one should examine the historical record on one's own time, and draw one's own conclusions.

To the Gnostics, the blind acceptance of Orthodox faith had reached a crossroad whereby the nuance of the Ark of the Covenant had weathered. Its golden veneer has been tarnished by the multitude that was unable to hold themselves to that high a standard. Understandably it was far easier to talk the talk than walk the walk. Consequently as the human being grew in awareness of his or her physical surroundings, and the circumstances of his or her physical life, a philosophical justification was sought for that awareness. The Gnostics considered they had reached that point of awareness unlike the Orthodox. This awareness yielded to a mutable expression of choice whereby one invested one's time and effort in the growth of his or her spiritual awareness. But the original charge had not changed in the interim. The onus was upon humankind to find the way to God; however one may perceive it, not the other way around. Noting the aura of celestial silence, it became apparent to the Gnostics, God intended the individual to find his or her own way through the wilderness, and not be led by nose as if one was a beast of the field. Being told what to think and how to think it was an unacceptable path to them, and they viewed the Orthodox as excelling in that process.

In their estimation, while what the Church Fathers offered a member of the congregation as one of the so-called faithfuls was questionable in value, what one gave in return was normally of tremendous personal value in the way of love, devotion, or material goods. It was clear the communicant stood to lose much more than the religious authority in this bargain. Promises of salvation and everlasting glory from those who were not empowered to give them were not just compensation for one's independence or material possessions. The Orthodox were able to accumulate their blessings without revealing their worth to the accountings of Man, but their true worth was revealed to God in their blasphemy. For this transgression, the Gnostics contended, the Orthodox would be held accountable in the hereafter when they were called to atone for their deeds. While the human being was easy to deceive in his eagerness to honor God, God could not be deceived; for ITS attitude was one of sublime patience. In the eyes of God, no human being could ultimately succeed in his or her deceptive practices; for the moment of judgment was inevitable though no human may live to see it. Though God had no personal interest in seeing justice done, the systemic influence of Universal Law would ensure ITS will would be done.

Unfortunately ideologies had been superimposed upon the faithful which defeated the purpose of understanding, and led to the misunderstandings of self, soul, and Spirit. As the self was muddied with material doctrines, it became increasingly difficult to separate the Truth from ideological biases. Invariably the ideology was substituted for the Truth, and when ideas were presented by an extraordinary individual, that individual would become identified with the ideas presented. Thus in time, all systems of belief had deteriorated into subtle or blatant forms of ego-worship because feelings faded and facts became distorted over time. Hence images of real people got replaced by caricatures, exaggerations of human qualities that no longer seemed accurate depictions of who they really were. Their ideas came to represent who they were for all eternity, and rightly or wrongly came to substitute for the substance of their character. Extrapolations upon ideology thus served as one's system of belief, and this contributed to a misunderstanding of how it came to be and what it ultimately meant.

However, the Orthodox Authority had been unable to fill-in-the-blanks of human life and the afterlife to the satisfaction of any reasoning individual. Furthermore no rational individual would promulgate theories of the afterlife as absolute certainties unless proof was at hand. While the Orthodox seemed to have little problem with it, it was in direct conflict with the rational approach of the Gnostic. The Orthodox tended to treat their mysteries as if they were certainties without a need for rational justification. Far and wide religious institutions tread heavily on the thin ice of myth and legend earnestly believing a convincing argument would eventually prove them right. Hence the lip-service paid to the congregation preyed upon the insecurities and naiveté of a populace which had the desire, but not the know-how. This vulnerability caused the anxieties with which humanity was afflicted that blocked a true understanding, namely, doubt, guilt, and fear. Orthodox faiths preyed upon those human deficiencies, and in return, the congregation was granted a guilt-repository to divest itself of responsibility for possessing them. But the relief was only a figment of imagination, and placebo for many enabling them to lead comfortable lives, notwithstanding their spiritual inadequacies. To the Gnostics, the problem was not the message being delivered. Truly it was the character of those who were delivering it.

If one fancied oneself a free-thinker as the Gnostics did, one could not rely upon the faith of the Orthodox congregation to supply the wisdom that was needed. Drinking from that trough discouraged understanding and encouraged the adoption of time-honored archetypes and propositions that contradicted the notion of free will. The spiritual highway of blind faith was littered with mysteries because the Orthodox faith had mystified their members to ensure their continuing allegiance. They excelled at supplying a modicum of wisdom at a time so that the parishioner must keep coming back for more. A superficial conviction required the reinforcement of a congregational consensus.

An external focal point like a priest, rabbi, imam, or minister was provided for the congregation whose function it was to mediate a connection to God. With a secondhand understanding of self, the actual meaning of God was blocked by the acceptance of sanctioned half-truths and untruths promoted by those who were supposedly authorized to know. These were assumed to have Gnosis, or knowledge, which enabled a spiritual understanding. But the facts the Gnostics saw did not support this supposition. In the majority of cases, they proved to be more knowledgeable, but no more enlightened than the individuals to which they ministered.

In actuality this observation was perfectly logical because the mediators were just people whose chosen profession was to minister to the needs of the congregation. The task was chosen by them, rather than them by God. No problem would arise if they were not held up to the Light by those to whom they minister; for in the Light one's defects became more pronounced. And once their flaws were noticed by those to whom they ministered, they were tolerated in so far as they did not reveal themselves to be hypocrites. If they were not expected to be stationed on a higher rung on Jacob's ladder than the common man, they might rest more at ease. In actuality, Orthodox clergy were not really held accountable for the traditional erroneous view of their respective station; unless they may choose to believe it, they were called by God to fill it.

In the Gnostic view, God called no one to serve HIM. It was a choice an individual made of one's own accord for the reasons for which only that individual was accountable. Furthermore God called no one to task unless it was one who had attempted to usurp HIS station. According to theological folklore, it would seem a fallen angel made a similar miscalculation of his self-importance in the eternal scheme of things, and suffered the consequences. As the Gnostics saw it, such was the fate of the one who coveted the throne.

Chapter 12 Sin And Absolution

While the Orthodox priest warned against sins of the flesh, the Gnostic teacher identified errors and taught how to correct them. The avoidance and denial technique promoted by the Orthodox was a way to handle temptation, and it caused many a guilty conscience or insatiable craving for a forbidden experience. Therefore many were left unfulfilled by their attempts at denial or their guilt for giving in to temptation. It was for this reason that Gnostics were encouraged to learn from their errors, so that they would not be repeated; for it was the repetition that constituted entrapment in a syndrome of bad behavior.

Because the Orthodox Christian did not feel safe without a safety net, a set of deterrents, the Ten Commandments, were borrowed from Judaism. Their purpose was to establish a behavior pattern for the practicing Christian that was utilized as a measuring stick for obedience. The Church conceived a role for itself as condemner and redeemer with the Sacrament of Penance. Closets were thrust open and skeletons placed inside, a reminder that the parishioner was an indentured servant of the Faith. Since sin was associated with nearly every carnal thought or act a human being might have, and those thoughts and deeds generally made people feel good, habitual sin became synonymous with a pleasurable material life. A psychological connection between purity and asceticism convinced most lay men and women that purity may not be possible for them. This decision was often reached before it could be tested.

The revolving door policy of sin-guilt-absolution kept the confessionals in business. It may have kept the parishioner's baser instincts in check, but it contributed nothing to his understanding. No sinful tendencies were rectified by confession unless it was accompanied by the recognition of error. Confession made it easier to rationalize sin by anticipating forgiveness for whatever sin was committed. The purpose could not have been corrective because only the symptoms were treated. As a result, the confession became very predictable in its ineffectual, indulgence-card absolutions. Virtue, the opposite of sin, was to imbue the congregation with hope that it would persevere against the ravages of sin despite all the evidence to the contrary. Nevertheless postulates of faith, hope and charity were the Truth no matter who believed them, and never were the sole possession of the churchgoer.

Would Man have learned to be virtuous without the

provocation of church regulation? The Orthodox insisted the flock required a Shepherd, implying Man would not be virtuous by choice. The Gnostic maintained that Virtue was not a by-product of church membership, but rather the result of a refined mind and pure heart. Therefore the Gnostic way was to assert that an individual must be virtuous by choice, and practice that virtuous behavior until it became ingrained by habit. Observance of the Golden Rule though praiseworthy was not sufficient to eradicate evil tendencies if it did not result in understanding what those tendencies were. Implicit in their analysis of good and evil, it seemed the Gnostics believed in the basic goodness of humankind, while the Orthodox believed the opposite. To them, Man was ripe for takeover by demonic forces, and the Universal Church existed to keep those forces at bay. The Gnostics argued Man could guard his own door if he or she knew how.

    Since the Orthodox faith stressed the worship of a God, a messiah, and adherence to the rules of the Church, it implied a member of the congregation need not understand how to do what must be done. The orthodox inferred the parishioner would evolve spiritually if he or she obeyed the rules, whether he or she understood them or not. It suggested the resulting class of spiritual automatons trusted their Faith because they were programmed for that response. Progress toward the goals of the Universal Church was measured by conformity to the rules and obedience, rather than knowledge. Their process of atonement was externalized to encompass the artificial reality of sin with Penance as the prescribed method to atone for deviations from the ordained path. The Gnostic process of *at-one-ment*, a concept borrowed from Judaism, was internalized to be the guardian of the path. When one knew what behavior to guard against, one was fully capable of recognizing error and remediating it themselves. Gnostics complained that Orthodox authority was far more demanding than God in its judgment, and exacting the punishment.

From *The Gospel of Mary*, a Gnostic text, date unknown, a savior emerged who renounced the prevailing Orthodox concept of sin. The text declared it to be a disturbance arising from an unnatural passion. The attitude displayed was more similar to Far Eastern principles of Harmony and Balance than to the prevailing Christian notions of Good versus Evil. After the resurrection, Yeshua appeared to his apostles and provided them with a game plan delivered during the Pentecost. The bone of contention between Gnostics and Orthodox was the substance of that game plan, not that there was one.

At the end of this dissertation on the concept of sin, Yeshua gave his apostles their charge. The Gnostics had their version. It appeared in the *Gospel of Mary* during the event called the Pentecost. *The Christ* admonished his apostles not to modify his teaching. He said, *"Go then and preach the gospel about the kingdom. Do not lay down laws beyond what I appointed for you nor make a law like the lawgiver, or else you'll be bound by it"*. Conversely the Orthodox had their version. At the beginning of ACTS OF THE APOSTLES, the incident called the Pentecost was recorded, *"But you will receive power when the Holy Spirit comes on you; and you will be my witnesses in Jerusalem, and in all Judea and Samaria, and to the ends of the earth (Acts of the Apostles 1:8)."* The Biblical verse did not contain the same warning about being the lawgiver that the charge in the Gospel of Mary contained.

Thus one could see the substance of the disagreements between Orthodox and Gnostic on the matter of the propagation of the faith. It also clarified how the Gnostics believed faith worked from the inside-out, rather than the outside-in. By their actions it also confirmed that the

Orthodox saw it the opposite way. The faithful had to be managed by rule and regulation, and they acted accordingly.

> Peter said to him, "Since you have explained everything to us, tell us this also: What is the sin of the world?" The savior said, "There is no sin, but it is you who make sin when you do things that are like the nature of adultery which is called 'sin'. That is why the Good came into your midst, to the essence of every nature, in order to restore it to its root." Then he continued and said, "that is why you [become sick] and die, for ... of the one who [... the who] under stands, let him understand. [Matter gave birth to] a passion that has no equal which proceeded from [something] contrary to nature. Then there arises a disturbance in the whole body. That is why I said to you, be of good courage, and if you are discouraged [be] encouraged in the presence of the different forms of nature. He who has ears to hear, let him hear." When the blessed one had said this, he greet ed them all saying, "Peace be with you. Receive my peace to yourselves. Beware that no one lead you astray, saying, 'Lo here! Or Lo there!' For the Son of Man is within you, Follow after Him! Those who seek will find him. Go then and preach the gospel of the kingdom. Do not lay down any rules beyond what I appointed for you, and do not give a law like the lawgiver lest you be constrained by it." When he had said this, he departed.

In its fragmentary form, *The Gospel of Mary* did not

reveal a complete picture of the savior. Much had been lost to interpretation or the decay of the original manuscript, but it presented a view consistent with Gnostic literature in general. What this text revealed were very different instructions from Yeshua that sent his apostles on their mission. The post-resurrection appearances of Yeshua to his disciples were common occurrences in Gnostic literature, as were references to error, karma, and reincarnation. In this text, however, the identity of Mary was not revealed. And whether the Mary cited in the gospel be Mary Magdalene, his consort, or Mary, his mother, was an arguable point of contention.

Certainly at greater issue were the divergent concepts of good and evil between Orthodox and Gnostic persuasions. The artificial struggle of good versus evil, concocted by the Orthodox, served to cloud the issue by masking the human struggle of metamorphosing the perverse substance into the sublime. The human conditions necessitating that process were immortal: the incessant sense of wonder, the desire to know the Creator, and the obsession with origin and conclusion. All of these influences necessitated a striving toward the point at which they coalesced in an earnest desire for compliance with the

Eternal Rule. That was an earnest desire for understanding, the goal of the Gnostics. The recognition of so-called evil was the recognition of harmony in and around an individual, a mirror-image of Yahweh's Ideal. The cause for disharmony was displayed in a dissatisfaction of self, an absence of purpose, and a feeling of insecurity bred by the intellectual and moral ambiguity posed by the vestiges of physical life.

The Gnostics taught that the void of morality manifested in the material ways of life was indicative of the reign of ego, and its stranglehold upon the commerce of humankind. The domination of ego led to institutionalized practices of selfishness, prejudice, and hatred in direct violation of every known spiritual precept. As long as the human being clung to these ego-doctrines believing they were true representations of spiritual principle, the contrived struggle of good versus evil would continue to dominate the intellectual landscape, and the journey of self-discovery would be driven off-course.

Hell then was defined by the failure to connect with the divine part of the human being, and one remained fixed in limbo until the connection was made. Heaven and hell were potential states of mind that were within reach always, and the choice of being in either state always rested with you.

Truly love was the way the connection was made, and if one failed to make that connection then only one was to blame for their lack. Heaven was realized when the connection was made and sustained. Otherwise one would linger in one's private hell until one gave in to love. No one would ever be punished sufficiently for their lack of compassion, but there was no need to dwell upon retribution; for the absence of love in one's heart was punishment enough.

In the Gnostic view, sins were errors of judgment, man-made and self-regulatory. Evil, the Gnostics maintained was not a force exerted from on high. It was an imbalance or discordant effect of Yahweh's Force. It was a perversion of Yahweh's Force within the human being, not exerted on humankind by an external force of evil. From THE AQUARIAN GOSPEL OF JESUS THE CHRIST in the *Conversation with the Magi of Persepolis*, was expressed a view on the nature of evil that was compatible with the Gnostics. It clearly elucidated the Gnostic view of good and evil hundreds of years after the Gnostic expression of the Christian faith had been obliterated by the Church. It presented the intriguing proposition that Man was a form of God. He created his own conception of good and evil, and the devil itself was a human invention.

[Jesus spoke to the magi, and said,] "I pray you, honoured masters, tell me how that evil can be born of that which is good?" A magus arose and said, "If you answer me, your problem will be solved. We all do recognize the fact that evil is. Whatever is, must have a cause, if God, the One, made not this evil then where is the God who did?" And Jesus said, "What ever God, the One, has made is good, and like the great first Cause, the seven Spirits all are good, and everything that comes from their creative hands is good. Now, all created things have colours, tones, and forms, [of] their own; but certain tones, though good and pure themselves, when mixed, produce inharmonies, discordant tones. And certain things, though good and pure, when mixed, produce discordant things, yes, poisonous things, that men call evil things. So evil is the inharmonious blending of the colours, tones, or forms of good. Now, man is not all-wise, and yet has willed his own. He has the power, and he uses it, to mix God's good things in a multitude of ways, and every day he makes discordant sounds, and evil things. And every tone and form, be it good, or ill, be comes a living thing, a demon, sprite, or spirit of a good or vicious kind. Man makes his devil thus; and then becomes afraid of him and flees. His devil is emboldened; follows his away and casts him into torturing fires. The devil and the burning fires are both the works of man, and none can put the fires out and dissipate the evil one, but the man who made them both."

Thus the Christ acknowledged that Man created his own sense of good and evil. He had the power to make either the joy or bane of his existence, or he had the power to make it go away. Therefore why would he not choose joy and forsake the sorrow forever? Certainly it was a question worth answering. Furthermore, why would a devil be assigned to act as adversary, when Man was so adept at tempting himself? Then further complicate the issue by punishing himself for his own transgressions? It was another question worth answering. The lesson to be learned was: whether one was a Gnostic or an Orthodox person of faith, the answers would all be different.

Chapter 13 The Role Of Women In Gnosticism

The role of women in Gnosticism was very similar to how they were treated in the Essene tribe. Throughout the centuries their treatment could be traced back to the dissimilar fates of four women, two mythical, and two actual historical women, but shrouded in mystery. However all of them could be considered legendary for different reasons. They have set the tone for the disposition of the Sacred Feminine throughout all of recorded history; the fortunes of which have wavered depending upon their expression in Patriarchal and Matriarchal Societies. One could argue Orthodox Christianity expressed the former while pagan Nature religions expressed the latter. These archetypes existed within the race memory of humanity, and were not so easily modified or erased. Thus Orthodox women for whom their religion was a rallying point in their respective lives were designated to be second-class citizens. Even the stout-hearted among them realized they had a mountain to climb. Conversely for Gnostic women, there was no gender stigma applied.

The first woman was Lilith. According to THE BOOK OF JUBILEES, the original story of Creation, she was Adam's first wife. Fragments of this book were found amongst the DEAD

SEA SCROLLS. Lilith was created as an equal partner out of the dust of the Earth like Adam. Their creation was detailed in GENESIS as follows. *"And the Lord God formed man of the dust of the ground. And breathed into his nostrils the breath of life; and man became a living soul" (Genesis 2:7).* Lilith was created in the same manner, making her an equal, and she acted the part. According to the legend, she was obstinate and would not submit to Adam's authority. Having a mind of her own, she would not obey his commands. Finally when Adam protested too much, she chose to go her own way. Eventually she abandoned him, blended into Nature, and became wild. The everlasting effect this legend had on Society at large was to characterize the female of the species as duplicitous, cunning, and domineering if they did not get their way. As time passed, the image of Lilith became more sinister and threatening, especially to children, as she was linked to the succubus. However such a designation was unwarranted for one who only wanted to express her individuality, and was not permitted to do so.

    The second was Eve, Adam's second wife, and the mother of mankind, whose fate was sealed by her role in the loss of paradise. Eve was created out of Adam's rib. Therefore the message was she was not an equal partner with Adam, but subordinate to him. According to biblical accounts, humanity was expelled from the figurative Garden of Eden because of her treachery, and Adam's complicity in the treachery. Although one could interpret that Adam was merely being supportive of his partner, he shared the blame for the expulsion from paradise, notwithstanding it was imposed by a jealous God. Although the story was a subject of legend, she was blamed for being the principal cause of humanity's fall from grace. It was partly because she was duped by the serpent into believing false claims of knowledge: that claim was to *become like God* as was promised by the serpent, and partly because she wanted to express her individuality, and decide for herself what she wanted to do.

The tree of knowledge was a symbol of awareness. In today's terminology, it would be defined as *woke*. The fulfillment of the desire for awareness however entailed a cost that was being responsible for one's own care and maintenance. Freedom and self-determination were a double-edged sword. With control came responsibility. In many respects, it was a mink-lined prison. Symbolic of this new awareness was the realization of nakedness for both Adam and Eve. In this sense, their nakedness symbolized a vulnerability to the elements of Nature and their newly-found separation from it. Certainly Eve's decision was a heavy burden to bear for all women who followed whether it be fact or fiction. The female gender never recovered from this mythical postulation. The everlasting affect was to add to that characterization of the female of the species – full of guile, deceitful and treacherous if given the opportunity. She was designated to be submissive to the male of the species, and the suggestion was if she was not, there was hell to pay as a consequence.

    The third was Mary the mother of Yeshua, the symbol of the virgin mother, meaning she was pure of heart, soul, and body. Because of that purity of Spirit she was the perfect vessel. It did not mean Mary was a virgin in a sexual sense. It was a carryover from Essene tradition. Though it was a contradiction in terms that a mother could be a virgin in a physical sense, her virginity was representative of the state of her soul more than the state of her body. It was pure unadulterated love in which Yeshua was formed and by which he was nurtured. Therefore it made perfect sense a master of his stature would emerge from it in a state of pure Virtue. In this state of being, with great lucidity and sublime love, Mary consecrated her child to Yahweh at the very moment he came into the world. Thus the archetype of the virgin accomplished the ancient rite of passage into the physical world. The secular vow of the Essene was to make the Word flesh in the pure vessel of the virgin. Thus the seed, being planted in fertile soil, nurtured by the community of Spirit, grew to become the savior of humankind. The opposite conditions would grow a human being to be its curse, an anti-Christ. This was the premise behind the symbolism of the anti-Christ, a product of the darkness of the human spirit. In other words, it was ego run amok, the very essence of sociopathic behavior whose yearn for self-aggrandizement knew no bounds.

The fourth was Mary Magdalene who according to Catholic tradition was deemed a prostitute who was saved by Yeshua from her life of wanton promiscuity. Gnostic tradition however presented her as a worthy disciple of Yeshua who was privy to his secret teachings, even offering the possibility that she was his life partner. For many Gnostics, she was an equal partner with the apostles who would never be seen to be on an equal standing because she was a woman. This was apparent by the stature she was accorded by Orthodox dogma. Most importantly when it came to his teachings, Yeshua did not withhold from her anything he would tell his apostles. It was even suggested by the Gnostic gospels; he confided in her more than them.

The same treatment of Mary Magdalene was not found in the dogma of the Universal Church. In their dogma, she was presented as the reformed prostitute, one who was saved from a life of sin and degradation by Yeshua himself. In fact they doubled down by making her also an adulteress. In the Universal Church, men were privy to knowledge that women were not. Men had the opportunity to serve as mediators to God in the priesthood, and women did not. The supposition was that women could not be trusted with knowledge because potentially they would turn out like Lilith. According to Orthodox tradition, such an eventuality would doom the human race.

Mary Magdalene's presentation as a prostitute was more a device to keep women subservient to men than it was a conscious effort to disparage the character of one woman. Character assassination was probably the best way to describe it. The Patriarchic overtones of the society in which Christianity was being preached was more to blame than the religion itself. By design it disparaged the character of all women, not as evil, but as incomplete specimens of humanity which allowed their emotional natures to predominant. Orthodox Christians merely followed the guidelines of the Patriarchal society to which they belonged. Conversely the Gnostics fought against it.

Passages from *The Gospel of Mary*, a Gnostic text from the 3rd century of the Common Era supported Mary Magdalene's special status. It alluded to the special relationship she had with Yeshua. However that relationship would be no different than one any man would have with his spouse, then or now. After the events of the resurrection, Peter said to her:

> *"Sister, we know that the savior loved you more than the rest of women. Tell us the words of the savior which you remember - which you know, (but) we do not nor have we heard them."*

The Gospel in question also noted that *"the savior often kissed her [Mary Magdalene] on the mouth"*. In this context, however, their relationship went beyond the mere bounds of pillow talk. She was involved in the mission and as such knew details his other disciples may not have been aware of. Peter even believed she had a special relationship with Yeshua that the rest of the apostles did not when he complained:

> "Did he [Yeshua] really speak privately with a woman (and) not openly with us? Are we to turn about and all listen to her? Did he prefer her to us?"

On Peter's part, evidence of the encroachment of patriarchic anxiety crept into this gospel. He could not believe that Yeshua would not prefer entrusting his message to men only, believing they would be the ones who would be carrying it to the world. It could be Yeshua's Essene training was showing. What was left unsaid by Peter was that women were not worthy to carry the message. But the crux of the matter lies in a statement Mary made to the apostles at the time of the Pentecost after they had received their charge to spread the word. It was:

> "Do not weep and do not grieve nor be irresolute, for His grace will be entirely with you and protect you. But rather let us praise his greatness, for he has prepared us (and) made us into men".

The question to pose would be: was Mary Magdalene's special status that of a consort or a disciple or both? The answer may be simpler than one would expect. Throughout the Gnostic gospels as well as the Synoptic gospels, the apostles addressed Yeshua as rabbi on many occasions. For all intent and purposes, Yeshua possessed the knowledge and experience to be considered to be a Jewish rabbi. Rabbis tended to instruct and guide members of their congregations. That was their job. Yeshua did exactly that with his apostles and disciples. Therefore to call him a rabbi was appropriate. Furthermore a rabbi was expected to be a family man, meaning he was supposed to take a wife and have children. That was the expectation of the Jewish community because he would be consulting members of the community on family matters. There's every reason to believe that Yeshua would have followed through on this requirement. That being the case, it was logical to assume that Mary Magdalene was his consort and disciple.

Considering the patriarchic nature of societies at the time, if Mary Magdalene was a disciple, she had to know her word would not be accepted simply because she was a woman. Thus it was left to the male disciples to preach the word of her consort, rather than her. It seemed her role was a mixture of Eve and Lilith, individualistic but supportive. She assumed the role of a coach, but not as a participant. Where she differed from Eve was the manner in which her partner-ship with Yeshua afforded her a prominent role in his mission. It was a big step up from the relationship between Adam and Eve in the Garden of Eden. One could only imagine the status of Essene women had a lot to do with that. Their influence on the Gnostic movement showed through in *The Gospel of Mary*. Women were equal partners in Creation.

On the other hand, the institutionalization of Orthodox religion has been the culprit in the creation of and perpetuation of the unfavorable sexual stereotypes under which the women of Western Civilization have labored for millennia. Those sexual stereotypes were aimed at maintaining their subservience. However thousands of years before the idea of equal opportunity for women was conceived, Gnosticism offered that possibility borrowing the concept from the Essene. The idea was linked to the mission of the savior, and the suggestion was given that Yeshua endorsed that notion. It was his intent that men and women were of equal stature in the kingdom of Yahweh. That's how the Essene saw it, and the Gnostics, in general, followed suit.

Orthodox Christianity, on the other hand, perpetuated unfavorable sexual stereotypes. They learned early on an easy way to control women and put them in a subservient role to men was to control the sexual behavior of men and women. Under the guise of faith, sexual behavior was categorized, dissected, and analyzed beyond any reasonable inquiry. In the Orthodox Christian view, sex was pronounced to be the province of satanic force, and those in its clutches were considered to be in league with the devil. Sex was considered to be something that should be licensed. As a sacrament called matrimony, sex was designated for married couples only, and any unauthorized use was forbidden. Offenders were threatened with excommunication which in olden days was akin to a sentence of spiritual death. Sexual stereotyping went so far as to enforce modes of behavior; for example, women were expected to control their feminine wiles and men their lecherous cravings. These behavior patterns conjured up images of pagan orgies of drunken debauchery and sexual misconduct which was fresh in the minds of early Christian converts. They had suffered through decades of pagan Roman sexual abuse when perversion was the norm.

Orthodox Christians were cognizant of the perversity of Roman sexual practices, heterosexual as well as homosexual. They attempted to forge a new sexual orientation from an earnest desire to escape a perverted past of pagan lust and lasciviousness. Ostensibly its purpose was to calm and redirect the selfish desires of humanity to a goal more satisfying than self-gratification. Furthermore it was justified as a method to overcome the scourge of the selfish desires of animal lust. Despite the altruistic notion of repressing what was considered to be deviant behavior, the over-zealous protectors of human sexuality went overboard in advocating the denial of sexual impulses. For them it was like applying the practice of fasting to the desire for human contact.

The Christian ideal of purity was derived from the teachings of Yeshua, but was not entirely the product of them. While he did advocate a virtuous state of being, he was not a fanatic. He did not demand its immediate acquisition, nor did he infer that less than virtuous meant inferior. Clear in his understanding that a virtuous life was the end result of a process of refinement, he did not leap to judgment of those who could not achieve it in a timely fashion. Furthermore he never condemned sexual intercourse unconditionally, and preached against promiscuity without condemning the promiscuous. To use Yeshua, aka Jesus of Nazareth, as an example of celibate purity as some have tried for millennia was ludicrous; for no one really knew if he in fact led a celibate life. It was a supposition made by the Orthodox who saw in his life's story, or what they think they knew of it, what they wished, and made their judgments accordingly.

What the Orthodox Christian practice of sexual denial presupposed was that sexual practices were an inherent polluter of the soul, because it caused one to love the body more than the soul. But the same was true for the love of money or of political power, and no Orthodox Christian seemed to be getting all bent out-of-shape over that, even though evidence of greed and corruption was rampant throughout Roman society. Sex seemed to stir the hornet's nest. The idea of sex as a pollutant was the product of minds obsessed with it. In attempting to deny themselves this earthly pleasure for the sake of purity, they postulated this denial, or abstinence, was fit for all.

The Gnostics taught there was evidence of disharmony in the spirited denial of anything. Moreover it was the recognition of this hypocrisy that had led to many losing faiths in the ambiguities of Orthodox religion. And to the contrary, when performed with the appropriate partner and the right attitude, where love was concerned, no physical act could be more uplifting emotionally. Many have been closer to God during orgasm, than sitting in a pew on Sunday, and apparently would not admit it.

Throughout the millennia, the Universal Church reinforced the idea that spiritual purity was juxtaposed with sexual activity. One's sexual appetite made the difference. Seemingly the greater the appetite, the further one drifted from any semblance of spirituality. What had not ever been said by Yeshua was that one could like having sex and still be pure of heart. They were not mutually exclusive. Furthermore no spiritual master had ever proposed that sex was inherently evil. The sum total of their collective teachings indicated that the fault lie in the wanton excess and perversion practiced by human beings. In the absence of virtue, egomania reigned. The Gnostic knew it all too well. The Orthodox knew it as well but misapplied the conclusion.

Chapter 14 The Issue Of Martyrdom

Martyrdom was one of the most decisive issues to spilt Orthodox and Gnostic Christians, and was perhaps the turning point of their tenuous relationship. While the Orthodox cherished the rapture of martyrdom, the Gnostics expounded upon the virtue of living one's faith. During times of social duress when Roman persecution of Christians was at its zenith, martyrdom was utilized as an example of the Christian will. The willingness to die for one's beliefs was certainly not a new idea, but this magnitude of mass murder/ genocide was unprecedented. To the Gnostic it represented the greatest of horrors, a forfeiture of the sacred gift of life for no good reason. Like lambs led to the slaughter, Orthodox Christians marched into the Coliseum imagining they were good Christian soldiers dying for a cause. Gnostics viewed this attitude as misguided naiveté personified in a waste of human life. Though diametrically opposed to following this example, they still bemoaned the loss of life.

However martyrdom was utilized by the Orthodox as a political lever to accelerate conversion to the Universal Church. Each new stone laid for the Church rested upon the bones of martyrs who proclaimed their sacrifice in the name of the Lord and Savior. Among the Orthodox, to die for one's faith became a source of pride, representing the ultimate sacrifice. They resented the Gnostics for their denunciation of martyrdom, and suggested the Gnostics were not steadfast in their faith because they avoided torture and death. The Gnostics retaliated by saying martyrdom was the only way the Orthodox had to prove their faith. Dying a horrible death, they maintained, did not contribute to the glory of the Christ. Its purpose only satisfied the perverse desires of the Church Fathers whose obsession with domination overrode any sense of Justice or Compassion. As far as the Gnostics were concerned, martyrdom was simply a forfeiture of life. Furthermore the compensation of eternal life in the Father was not deemed to be fair compensation, since it was available anyway to ones who exhibited a purity of character and virtue. The Orthodox, they maintained, treated martyrdom as if it was an override for a life of sin. They implied a blood sacrifice was sufficient to grease the path to heaven, and it did not matter what one had done previous to that. Their sins were expunged by that blood sacrifice. Presumably they modeled after the initial blood sacrifice of Yeshua at the hands of Jewish and Roman authorities. The Gnostics did not seek to emulate the Christ in that manner preferring a life of virtue to a sacrificial death.

Be assured however there was only a fleeting glory in martyrdom. A forfeiture of one's life was not just compensation for any cause. Murder was murder by any standard without qualification so says the Law of Moses. But this Law was sullied by the actions of the children of Israel who systematically slaughtered the residents of the land of Canaan, truly believing they were following the commandment of Jehovah. The order to be fruitful and multiply in the Promised Land did not necessarily mean at the expense of those who currently occupied it.

The height of irony perhaps was symbolized by where the early Christian faith was practiced in Rome. At the hands of persecution by pagan Roman authorities under Nero, Christians were driven underground into the catacombs beneath the city of Rome. There they could practice their faith in secrecy and safety away from the scrutiny of imperial jurisdiction. It was likely they were influenced by and eventually adopted some of the symbolism of the previous inhabitants of those catacombs.

In these catacombs, the followers of the pagan god Mithras sought refuge centuries before. Mithras was a principal angelic deity of Zorasterism which originated in

Persia. As a deity, it presided over covenant and oath. In addition to being the divinity of contracts, Mithras was also a judicial figure, an all-seeing protector of the Truth, a guardian of cattle, and the harvest. Being a guardian of the water, it was its charge to ensure the pastures and livestock received enough of it. Mithras was symbolized by the primeval bull and was also associated with the sun. Mithraism had migrated from the Middle East centuries before to take up residence in Rome, Greece, and the rest of Asia Minor.

As the Roman expression of Mithraism developed, it grew away from its roots in Persian mythology. Mithras came to symbolize something different in Rome. It literally became the divinity of the Sun. Ironically there were a long list of attributes Mithras shared with the character and personality of the Messiah. For example, Mithras was born on December 25th of the virgin Anahita. The babe was wrapped in swaddling clothes, placed in a manger, and attended by shepherds. Mithras was considered a great traveling teacher and master. He had twelve companions or disciples who traveled with him. On these travels, he performed miracles. As the great bull of the sun, Mithras sacrificed himself for world peace, and ascended to heaven.

He was viewed as the Good Shepherd and was proclaimed, *the way, the truth and the light, the redeemer, the savior, and the messiah.* To adherents, Mithras was omniscient, indicating he heard all, saw all, knew all, and none could deceive him. He was identified with both the lion and the lamb. His sacred day was Sunday, the Lord's Day, hundreds of years before the appearance of the Christian messiah. His religion had a Eucharist or Lord's Supper. It emphasized baptism, love, and compassion. To identify defenders of the true faith of Mithras, his soldiers had marks set on their foreheads. The similarities with Christianity were too many to be a coincidence, so many it would be challenging to tell them apart.

The irony lies in migration from sun to son. It appeared that in the transference of attributes between Mithras and Yeshua, *Sun of God* became *Son of God*. In retrospect, it was a transition that might have been purely psychological, so that few were aware of it. Nonetheless the coincidence was striking, and the translation of myths one to the other was a human tradition. To rejuvenate time-honored archetypes, myths were simply reformulated, re-purposed, and reassigned.

For the Orthodox Christians, these reformulated

archetypes and myths gave them something to die for, above and beyond love of God and his son. They dutifu ly marched into the Coliseum and laid down their lives, staining the sand red with their blood before lions and gladiators. Those martyred envisioned it to be their pathway to heaven. They were thinking all the time: it was their salvation. The Gnostics watched in dismay at the waste of human life.

Chapter 15 The Politics Of Power

An ideological power struggle ensued between Orthodox and Gnostic which centered upon the location of the seat of temporal church authority. For centuries influential Gnostics such as Simon Magus and Clement of Alexandria had challenged the authority assumed by the Universal Church as heir apparent to Peter. Throughout Asia Minor, Orthodox bishops claimed a right of inheritance from the apostles that excluded the Gnostics unless they submitted to Roman authority. This right of inheritance was predicated upon the transfer of power from Peter to his successors in Rome. The belief was that each would preside over the body of the Church in Peter's stead. Peter's lineage was an arguable point as was his special authenticity since each apostle was charged with the same purpose at the Pentecost.

The supposition of Peter's authority was founded upon a verse from the Gospel of Matthew when Yeshua reportedly said "*You are Peter, and upon this rock, I will build my church. I will give you the keys to the kingdom, and whatever you bind on Earth will be bound in heaven (Matthew 16:18-19).* This reference did not appear as definitive in any recently discovered Gnostic literature. Neither was there any confirming reference in the Canon to this rock except in that one verse. The Gnostics contended that such a determination was made after the fact to validate Roman authority.

The Gnostics argued that those who assumed authority in the Universal Church were in many cases unqualified for the positions they occupied. Their disqualification was displayed by their materialism and lust for power. The rule of virtue for which the Christ had championed, Gnostics contended, was being turned into a mockery. The unworthy held sway and oppressed the faithful with their rule. To this day, the Eastern Orthodox Church denied Peter's authority.

Needless to say, the Orthodox notion of Peter's special status did not sit well with many of the Gnostic sects. It was inferred that if Peter had traveled to Athens, the pope would sit there instead. The Church which the Master had envisioned, Gnostics argued, was one of the Spirit that was manifested within humanity. Such a church would be founded upon divine principles of Love, Compassion, and Brotherhood, and not be the legacy of one man however impressive. They vigorously protested the Orthodox right of inheritance claiming no man could assume corporal leadership of a spiritual church. Such leadership, they argued, would result in religious despotism. Peter, they claimed, was chosen by the church fathers because he was a celebrity who preached in Rome, the ruler of the ancient world. His qualifications for the job were no more noteworthy than any of the other apostles. Much of their ministry had simply been lost in the mists of Time.

The following passages were taken from the *Apocalypse of Peter*, a Gnostic document of anonymous origin, circa 250 CE. It described the Gnostic rationale for opposition to Orthodox authority. The words it contained were presented as the actual words of the Logos, Yeshua the Christ spoken to his disciples.

> *"And when I said these things", the Savior said, "I have told you that these [people] are blind and deaf now then, listen to it things which I tell you in a mysery, and guard them. Do not tell them to the sons of this age; for they shall blaspheme you in these ages since they are ignorant of you, but they will praise you in knowledge; for many will accept our teaching in the beginning. And they will turn from them again by the will of the father of their error, because they have done what it wanted. And it will reveal them in his judgment as the servants of the word. But those who became mingled with these shall become their prisoners, since they are without perception. And the guileless, good, pure One they push to the worker of death, and to the kingdom of those who praise Christ in a restoration. And they praise the men of the*

propagation of falsehood, those who come after you. And they will cleave to the name of a dead man, thinking that they will become pure. But they will be come greatly defiled, and they will fall into the name of Error, and into the hand of an evil, cunning man and a manifold dog ma, and they will be ruled heretically. For some of them will blaspheme the truth and proclaim evil teaching. And they will say evil things against each other."

"But many others who oppose the truth and are the Messengers of Error, will set up their error and their law against these pure thoughts of mine; as looking out from one [perspective], thinking that good and evil are from one [source]. They do business in my word, and they will propagate a harsh fate."

The ambivalent wording of this segment of the *Apocalypse of Peter* permitted its use by both sides in rhetorical attacks upon the other. The true meaning, however, must be interpreted within the heart of the interpreter; for in this way only will the truth of this statement ever be realized. In the light of true understanding, the inherent fallibility of the written word becomes clear. The Apocalypse continued with a prophecy of the fate of the counterfeit ones who oppressed the little ones of limited intellect. From the Gnostic point of view, the messengers of error became prominent in the Church in 4th century of the Common Era when Constantine became emperor.

"And there shall be others of those who are outside our number who name themselves bishops and deacons; as if they have received their authority from Yahweh. They bend themselves under the judgment of the leaders. Those people are dry canals." But I [Peter] said, "I am afraid because of what you [Yeshua] have told me; that indeed the little ones are in our view, the counterfeit ones. Indeed, that there are multitudes that will mislead other multitudes of living ones, and destroy them among themselves. And when they speak your name, they will be believed. "The Savior said, "For a time determined for them in proportion to their error they will rule over the little ones. And after the completion of the error, the never aging one of immortal understanding shall be come young, and they [the little ones] shall rule over those who are their rulers. The root of their error they shall pluck out, and they shall put it to shame so that it shall be manifest in all the impudence which it has assume to itself. And such ones shall be unchange able, O Peter."

From the Gnostic perspective, the Universal Church, while serving the need some had to be authoritative, did not succeed in instilling the spiritual church in its members. No matter what heritage it claimed, the Universal Church failed in most cases to improve the inner man. In those cases where an individual achieved his best within the Church, it was not a beneficial effect of Church membership, but instead was the results of the individual's purity and insight. The soul of man, Gnostics intimated through their writings, was unnoticed and unmoved. This was because its effort was aimed at manipulating the outer-shell of a man into a posture of obedience. Hence its teachings were geared toward whipping up an orderly, socially-conscious, though spiritually-deprived congregation into a homogeneous substance. A false hierarchy of God-priest-parishioner was instituted to achieve this aim, with a priest class administering to the faith of thousands in observance of a prescribed canon. Orthodox wisdom was imparted to the masses from the pulpit as gospel history and observance of the Golden Rule. Since the Orthodox relied heavily upon the Scriptures to validate their faith, their dogma became a tool to adjust the screws upon humanity.

The Universal Church slowly evolved into more of a government than a religious expression, arbitrating God's Laws among men. The Gnostics claimed, they legislated their own laws, created sacraments, and instituted rituals designed to mimic a life of virtue without attaining it. The congregation was hereby deluded into a false sense of spiritual security in vain accomplishments. This was partly due to the fact the real accomplishments of Yeshua were a mystery to the uninitiated, particularly his affiliation with the Essene tribe. Much of his development as the Messiah may have been unknown to those with whom he interacted including the apostles.

Consequently the teachings of the Christ were split into exoteric and esoteric versions by the Orthodox. Church congregations were presented with a commercialized, paint-by-it-numbers brand of Christianity which could be practiced simply. This brand became Catholicism with its stone buildings to symbolize the living church as the Orthodox saw it. The esoteric meanings of Christian philosophy were saved for the initiated few within the Catholic hierarchy.

Gnostics watched the development of the Universal Church with growing concern, bemoaning the spiritual deprivation of its participants. Gnostics were summarily denounced by the Orthodox for their renegade belief systems which varied throughout the Mediterranean theater of operation. A priest class, Gnostics responded, would only serve to apply a needless filter upon the Light of God, and many would fall into the clutches of error.

As Roman persecution was relaxed, the Orthodox and Gnostic traditions grew further apart in theory and practice. As the Universal Church grew in size its influence increased. While the Church extended its domain, the

Gnostic movement remained fairly static in size and influence. No sect arose to unite the others and join together in a concerted political effort because that was not their way. Small bands of practicing Gnostics persisted in their individual rural or urban communities basically incommunicado. The introverted style of the Gnostics lent credence to Orthodox claims of heresy in the minds of the uniformed. Their secret-society attitude led to their undoing because it was eventually used by the Orthodox to validate accusations of conspiracy to undermine the so-called true Church.

Chapter 16 The Nicene Creed

As the Universal Church grew the problem of standardizing the Orthodox faith became more acute, and the need to centralize and organize its power structure became more obvious. Those in power realized the need to safeguard that authority, both in theory and in practice. The Catholic authority then recognized the need to establish a Canon which all church members would share, no matter where they lived. Thus the conflict with the Gnostics came to a head.

Recognizing the need to standardize the Faith in light of the prevailing Gnostic and pagan threat, an ecclesiastical conference was called in 325 CE to address the perceived problem. This forum was the Nicene Council at which were assembled the ruling bishops from each Christian locale in the known world. Responding to what was perceived as a mission to preserve the true Faith, the Church Fathers launched a centuries-long campaign to eradicate the Gnostic and pagan menace, as they saw it, to their expression of Faith. Even though it was known Gnostics were Christians, their ideology was substantially different than the Orthodox Christians. The threat they posed was also substantially different. Thus they were lumped into the same category as pagans. The Nicene Creed proved to be an invaluable tool for identifying and combating heresies of all kinds, and for putting pagans in their place.

The typical pagan, a Latin derivative meaning country-dweller, was illiterate and mainly populated rural areas. The term, pagan, should not be applied to non-Christian urbanites because the word did not fit the definition. The non-Christian urbanites differed from the country-dwellers in perspective as well as practice due to the practical necessities of their respective lives, mainly because they were literate. In the pre-institutional model of Christian Authority, urbanites were paired with a local clergy. The faith of the community was endorsed by the civil authority, and administered by a clergy that was an extension of that authority. The esoteric matters of the faith were left to the discretion of the local clergy who were deemed experts in the interpretation of church law. The actions of the populace were judged upon moral and civil grounds by essentially the same Authority.

The main issue at the Nicene Council proved to be the human/divine controversy of the nature of the Christ. In essence the dispute was over whether or not Yeshua, the man, was human or divine. This debate had been raging for decades. The denial of the divinity of the Christ, proposed by a Gnostic teacher named Arius, was hotly contested by the Orthodox Christian champion, Athanasius. A great debate ensued during which the anger and frustration of both sides of the argument was vented. When the dust had settled, Arianism had been declared a heresy.

The Nicene Creed which was roughly equivalent to a constitution of the Church was issued to establish the body of the Universal Church and summarize its teachings. The Nicene Creed was a statement of Faith and a pledge of allegiance to the Universal Church. It read as follows:

> *I believe in one God,*
> *the Father Almighty*
> *maker of heaven and earth*
> *and of all things visible and invisible.*
> *I believe in one Lord Jesus Christ,*
> *the only begotten son of God,*
> *born of the Father before all ages.*
> *God from God, Light from Light,*
> *True God from true God,*
> *begotten, not made, consubstantial with the Father;*
> *Through him all things were made.*
> *For us men and for our salvation*
> *he came down from heaven,*
> *and the Holy Spirit was incarnate of the Virgin Mary,*
> *and became man.*
> *For sake he was crucified under Pontius Pilate,*
> *he suffered death and was buried,*
> *and rose again on the third day*
> *in accordance with the Scriptures.*

*He ascended into heaven
and is seated at the right hand of the Father.
He will come again in glory
to judge the living and the dead and his kingdom will
have no end.
I believe in the Holy Spirit, the Lord, the giver of life,
who proceeds from the Father and the Son, who with
t*

*he Father and the Son is adored and glorified, who
has spoken through the prophets. I believe in one,
holy, catholic and apostolic Church. I confess one
Baptism for the forgiveness of sins and I look forward
to the resurrection of the dead and the life of the
world to come. Amen.*

The Nicene Creed was a statement of unification which mandated a sanctioned version of the Canon. It was approved by all of the bishops except the one representing Alexandria, Egypt. That jurisdiction had been operating autonomously for decades. The disagreement in policy, however, was motivated for reasons of doctrinal conflict. Clearly this demarcated the Egyptian Christians from the remainder of Christendom. It put the spotlight on other issues of faith which were the seat of temporal church authority, pantheism, the nature of the Christ, and reincarnation. Also it intensified a competitive philosophical antagonism between Alexandria and Rome, and then Constantinople which simmered for decades before erupting into violence.

The emperor, Constantine the Great, who had issued the Edict of Milan in 313 CE proclaiming official tolerance of all religions, staunchly supported the edicts issued from Nicaea though he was pagan. Most likely his motivation was in promoting peace and stability in his empire. Through the imperial benefactor, his mother, who had previously converted to Christianity, the Universal Church prospered socially and economically. Privileges were accorded the Church in the form of political favors and public funds, and Christianity spread like wildfire through the pagan urban class. Although he only became a Christian on his deathbed, Constantine left an empire increasingly animated by a sense of Christian solidarity. That solidarity was understandably of the Orthodox variety.

When the Egyptian Christians objected to the Roman adoption of Catholicism as the state religion, they were effectively censured in the Christian world. Their argument was that it would prove to be an inherent conflict of interest to identify God and Caesar as one. When the fish began appearing on Roman coins opposite the image of Caesar, the affairs of the Church became the concern of the State. Before Christianity officially adopted the Christian model of Authority in the 6th Century of the Common Era, pagan was redefined in contrast to Christian so that political distinctions could be drawn between them. Pagan was thus identified as non-Christian to facilitate the creation of an us versus them mentality. Judaism retained its individuality. Primarily it was seen as the precursor to Christianity. Hence the phrase Judeo-Christian was coined and utilized for historical purposes.

Major parts of the Canon were in essence copies of Jewish books that the Orthodox Christians commandeered like the Torah, books of the Jewish prophets, Psalms, Ben Sira or Ecclesiastes, and various books of Jewish history. These constituted the Old Testament. Typically these were the ones that did not introduce controversial topics into the Canon. Controversial Jewish doctrine like the BOOK OF JUBILEES or the BOOK OF ENOCH was excluded from the Old Testament portion of the Canon.

THE BOOK OF ENOCH was a Jewish apocryphal text in five parts in which the main character Enoch, the great-great-grandfather of Noah, ascended into heaven and conversed with the angels. One of these angels, named Uriel, guided Enoch on a journey through the seven levels of heaven, and instructed him on the ways of the angels. Enoch was given knowledge concerning the Cosmos, the

Natural world, and the nature of God to which, he believed, only the angels of the Lord were privy to at the time. In our day and age, this information would equate to a rudimentary education in the sciences of geology, astronomy, physics, mathematics, and biology. At one time the book was widely read by Christians, and was an integral part of Hebrew tradition. After the Council of Nicaea circa 325 CE, it was declared to be heretical and excised from the canon.

Now the reasons for its exclusion were a matter of conjecture. The reference to the historical personage of Enoch in **Genesis** was relegated to a two-liner. *"Enoch walked with God, and he was no more, for God took him" (Genesis 5: 21-24).* If one was to believe what was written in the tome of Enoch, of which there were five books, ostensibly written by his hand, there was much more to the story. This knowledge was deliberately withheld from Orthodox Christians. Presumably that was because it presented topics that the Universal Church did not want their members to delve into. It raised questions they had no answers for, particularly the genealogy of the human race.

In actuality, a footnote should have been placed in Genesis to indicate that the books of Enoch existed. Then humanity could be advised if one wished to investigate forgotten pages of history, discarded by the Universal Church, one had the opportunity to do so. Labeling it apocryphal (another word for speculative) and hiding it away only served the interest of ideologies which strove to keep the knowledge it contained from prying eyes. Both THE BOOK OF ENOCH and THE BOOK OF JUBILEES were excluded from the Christian canon at the same time. Whether keeping the knowledge they contained secret served the purpose of keeping it out of the hands of those who would abuse it, or spoke to the motives of the powers-that-be. These motives served the belief that knowledge should be kept under lock and key. The reason for secrecy at this point was purely speculative.

But if history taught one anything, it was that knowledge was power. The reader may take from that what he or she will, concerning the motivations of the powers-that-be of the Universal Church. However, the subject matter contained in the aforementioned banned books concerned topics that the Universal Church intended to suppress. Basically it had little to do with Christianity as such but rather events or subjects in pre-history that the Universal Church preferred not to deal with. They did that by not acknowledging these events even happened. These were topics beyond the scope of their religious doctrine for the most part. Therefore their exclusion from the Canon did not spark much controversy, Some of these events will be discussed in a future chapter concerning the history of THE CHILDREN OF THE LAW OF ONE.

At the conference in Nicaea, the main sticking point between Bishops on doctrine was the establishment of the New Testament portion of the Canon. Mainly that Canon contained the four gospels, ACTS OF THE APOSTLES, thirteen epistles of Paul, book of Hebrews, 1 Peter, 1 John, and REVELATION. In all, it represented twenty-two books. The books that were disputed were 2 Peter, Jude, James, and 2 and 3 John as well as the Gnostic gospels of Philip, Thomas, Mary, Peter, Nicodemus, and the Epistles of Ignatius and Clement, among others. These Gnostic gospels introduced controversial subjects like reincarnation, pantheism, Neo-Platonism, the role of women in Christianity, and the family of Yeshua. These and other topics were deemed heretical by the Universal Church. The Church did not wish to discuss any of these topics because some of them called into question the very foundations of the Church itself, and how the Universal Church came to be in the first place. Moreover when one did not have a response to the charges being levied, one simply refused to respond.

The Canon was utilized to identify the true believer in relation to the pagan confederate. In the process, regarding doctrine, the Gnostics were lumped into the pagan category. Due to their multiplicity of pagan influences, and secret society leanings, it was easy to do so. As Alexandria lost allies in the struggle of determining Christian doctrine, its weakened position at the bargaining table was next.

Chapter 17 Monophystism Versus Dyophystism

Over the ensuing decades, the arguments over the dual nature of the Christ heated up. By the middle of the 4th Century of the Common Era, Egyptian Gnosticism was the dissenting view in an increasingly Orthodox Christian world. Valentinus who represented a large Gnostic following at this time, and a group of teachers from the Catechetical School supported a Monophysite view of the nature of the Christ. They declared Yeshua, the man, through his intellect and soul exhibited the Christ Consciousness. This view was opposed by the remainder of Orthodox Christianity, including the authorities at Rome and Constantinople who proposed a dual nature instead. They proposed Yeshua the man was distinctly separate from his identification as the Christ. The proof they maintained was that the miracles he performed could not have been performed by a man. When the Christ emerged, they declared, the man, Yeshua was consumed.

Hard-core Orthodox bishops like Irenaeus used the single/dual controversy to launch rhetorical attacks upon the Egyptian and Syrian Gnostics. He railed against the pagan Classical influence exhibited by the Catechetical School, claiming it had been corrupted with the intellectual delusions of pagan philosophies. His assault on its reputation within the

Christian community of Alexandria called for the expulsion of the Gnostics from the school and the community. Orthodox moderates like Tertullian, an early Christian scholar and historian, advocated censure of the school and proposed reformation of its activities. Reformation in his opinion was a compromise with official Church policy to water-down the radical ideas of Gnosticism.

In 360 CE, Athanasius, then bishop of Alexandria, had been appointed by Church authorities to purge the Gnostics. He wrote an Easter letter condemning the heretics and "*their apocryphal books to which they attribute the names of saints*". Because the Manichean sects or their literature were influencing the Pachomian monastic movement, the Abbott of these monasteries, Theodore, had the letter translated into Coptic and posted in each monastery. Athanasius's reference to the Nag Hammadi codices did not name a specific text, but this proved they were in circulation and influential. However, the subsequent closing of the school and its library by Orthodox Christians late in the 4th Century of the Common Era seemed to be a more effective blow to the preservation of the Gnostic heritage than any letter. At the same time, it served notice to pagans that their ways would not be tolerated either. The supposition was that the Nag Hammadi codices were hidden in caves near selected monasteries prior to the closing of the Catechetical School. In the manner that the Gnostics had hid their manuscripts from the conquering pagan Romans in the 2nd Century of the Common Era, the Gnostic scholars likely anticipated the scourge of the Roman Christians, and transported their texts to sympathetic monks for safe-keeping lest they be destroyed.

The ultimate irony which exposed the folly of the early Orthodox Christian heresy-hunters occurred in 385 CE. It was highlighted by the efforts of the heresy hunters to undermine pagan Classicism and Gnostic ideology consisted of temple sackings and pillaging throughout the Roman theaters of occupation. One such event had been recorded centuries earlier by the perpetuator himself, the emperor Theodosius in his edict, *De Idolo Serapidis*. This edict was issued for the expressed purpose of exterminating pagan philosophy in Alexandria, Egypt, and was specifically aimed at the followers of Serapis.

This deity was revered in Greece as well as Egypt under different names, but all symbolized the embodiment of wisdom and strength. However as Christianity spread through the multitudes of Alexandria, Serapis became increasingly associated with the Christ. The association became so much so that in the 2nd Century the emperor Hadrian, while traveling in Egypt, wrote to Servianus who was an Iberian Roman Senator. Hadrian declared, *"The worshippers of Serapis were Christians, and even their bishops worshipped at his (Serapis) shrine."* A witness to the sacking of the temple of Serapis which was attached to the Library at Alexandria echoed the sentiment of Hadrian.

> *When the Christian soldiers, in obedience to this order (De Idolo Serapidis), entered the Serapeum at Alexandria to destroy the image of Serapis which had stood there for centuries, so great was their veneration for it that they dared not touch it image lest the ground should open at their feet and engulf them. At length, overcoming their fear, they demolished the\statue, sacked the building, and finally as a fitting climax to their offense burned the magnificent library which was housed within the lofty apartments of the Serapeum. Several writers have recorded the remarkable fact that Christian symbols were found in the ruined foundations of this pagan temple. Socrates, a Church historian of the 5th century, declared that after the pious Christians had razed the Serapeum at Alexandria and scattered the demons who dwelt there under the guise of Gods, beneath the foundations was found the monogram of Christ.*

The inevitable showdown between Alexandria and Rome on the issue of the nature of the Christ occurred at the

Council of Chalcedon in 451 CE. During the ensuing debate, both adversaries exhausted their patience and vented frustrations of the two centuries of philosophical conflict. Against overwhelming odds, the Egyptian Gnostics had swayed the Council to see it their way successfully at the previous two councils in Ephesus. This time Rome prevailed. Monophysitism was declared to be a heresy, and the Egyptian patriarch, Dioscorus, was sent into exile. Nonetheless the decisions of Chalcedon were never accepted by the Egyptian Church, and mob violence ensued in Alexandria. From this point onward, the philosophical struggle turned bloody in Egypt as Christian fought Christian, as Christian had fought pagan.

Chapter 18 Gnostics In The Crosshairs

After the Councils of Nicaea and Chalcedon, the Universal Church gained a widespread recognition and acceptance of its creed. With the installment of Catholicism as the state religion of the Roman and Byzantine Empires, the inner-directed ways of the Gnostic Christians fell into official disfavor. Radical ideas such as reincarnation and pantheism were repudiated as heretical. All Gnostics comprising the range of Gnostic sects like the Simonians, Manicheans, Valentinians, and Neo-Platonists, to name a few were socially ostracized at the very least. Labeled as outlaws they were a short step away from persecution for their beliefs like any other undesirable minority group in any Age.

The Bishop of Cyprus, Epiphanius, to whom a cook book on combating heresy of all kinds was attributed, wrote of an encounter with Egyptian Gnostics. His attitude typified the Orthodox perspective of the 4th and 5th centuries which associated Gnosticism with the devil. This correlation was motivated by the Orthodox fervor to expose and extinguish what was perceived to be a menace to the so-called faithful. The judgmental attitude displayed in his reaction to the Gnostics showed no depth of understanding or compassion toward those who worshipped differently. To the contrary, he acted with an Old Testament attitude when adversaries were hated and feared, and allies were loved and embraced. The New Testament attitude by contrast should be to love one and all regardless. However, it was this demonstration of abject bigotry that truly represented the mindset of the typical Orthodox zealot.

> *I have had a brush with this sect [Egyptian Gnostic] myself, beloved, and got my information about its customs in person, straight from the mouths of its members. Women who believed this nonsense offered it to me, and told me the kind of thing I have been describing. In their brazen impudence, what is more, they tried to seduce me, like that vicious, wicked Egyptian woman who was married to the chief cook. I was young, and this made me attractive to them. For the women who told me about this salacious myth were outwardly very charming, but all the devil's ugliness was in their vile minds. However, the merciful God saved me from their depravity. When while I was at it, I read their books, understood what they really intended, and was not entrapped as they had been; their literature left me unmoved. And I promptly reported these people to the local bishops, and found which of them were masquerading as members of the Church. And so they were driven out of the city, about eighty of them, and it was cleansed of their rank, thorny growth.*

Those practicing outlawed Christianity were initially excommunicated from the Universal Church. Ironically it was a Church to which most never belonged. If the illegal practices persisted, those responsible were banished from the Christian community at large, or even the municipality where they lived. Repeat offenders were sometimes put to death, but that treatment varied with the attitude of the territorial bishop directing the persecution. Some were more fanatical than others, but as the persecutions persisted over the ensuing decades, the fanatical grew in number, and the attack upon the Gnostics became more violent. It soon became official Church policy to deny that the Gnostics were Christian in any way.

They were additionally charged, in absentia, with permitting the true faith of the Orthodox persuasion to be contaminated with pagan ideas. These influences that Orthodox saw as contamination came from the incorporation of Egyptian, Persian, Syrian, Hindu, and Neo-Platonic traditions. The Gnostics responded that the charges of contamination were ludicrous, and argued Yeshua himself had made numerous references to reincarnation, karma, and the Creative life of the Soul in his teachings. These had been excised from the Canon at the insistence of the Orthodox majority during previously mentioned Councils. This argument was vehemently denied by Church authorities who viewed any such interpretations as further evidence of Satan's attempts to destroy the True Church under the guise of Gnosticism. Gnostics themselves were pronounced to be the agents of satanic forces which sought to undermine the Church. Using this psychological ploy, all sympathy or pity of the populace could be denied the Gnostics since they were associated with the avowed enemy of humankind. It became a mortal sin to associate with Gnostic Christians in any way, economically or socially. They were ostracized by every part of Society under the auspices of the moral authority of the Universal Church.

By the time the Gnostics realized the seriousness of their crimes against Church authority, it was too late to compromise. It became necessary for Gnostics to hide from Orthodox persecution, much the same way that all Christians had under the persecution of the pagan Roman rulers like Nero. Gnostics who survived carried on their particular traditions in secrecy. Many joined the Universal Church so that their affiliation with the radical Gnostic underground would not be discovered. Others who stubbornly clung to their Gnostic roots reformed into smaller bands that practiced in secluded locales. Secret societies of Gnostics that once practiced in the sunlight operated nocturnally giving rise to superstitious gossip of bizarre midnight ceremonies and strange rites of passage. Because of being forced to practice in sylvan locales, the Gnostics became synonymous with the ideologies and methodologies of pagan mystery schools in the minds of the Orthodox. It was easy to make outlandish accusations of Satan worship from the pulpit against those who were not in attendance. Deprived of the right to publicly express their faith without risking life and limb, Gnostics withdrew to safety because martyrdom was not their way. As time went on, this withdrawal resulted in dramatic changes in Church leadership throughout North Africa.

Augustine, the Bishop of Hippo, a city in North Africa, presented in his work, THE CITY OF GOD, a lone dissenting view in the new Church formula of identification with the Roman Empire. He rejected its imposition upon the spiritual awareness of the Christian. Unfortunately his opinion mattered little to the power-seekers of the Roman and Byzantine churches who envisioned no challenge to their authority. Even though he was later canonized for the sincerity of his life's work, his concern for the vacuum of material Christianity was shelved along with his book.

The final blow to Gnostic Christianity was dealt by the

emperor Justinian and his consort Isadora in the 6th century of the Common Era. They spearheaded a movement to complete the Christianizing of the Roman and Byzantine empires. Conspiring with a willing accomplice in a papal legate named Pelagius, they used Christianity as an excuse to remake the Empire in their image. Justinian issued codes of ethics and revised civil laws, while Isadora allocated public tax funds for the construction of cathedrals and shrines.

Pelagius engineered a key ecclesiastical conference to reaffirm the mandate of the Nicene Creed. For his part in the conspiracy, Pelagius was awarded the papacy when a weak-willed pope, Vigilis, failed to do the bidding of the emperor, so much for the separation of Church and State. Thus the specter of a Holy Roman Empire finally became a reality under the reign of Justinian and Isadora.

Cut-off ideologically from the remainder of Christendom, the Egyptian Christian Church persisted until circa 641 CE, when Egypt was conquered by Arab tribes. Expectedly the Arabs did nothing to preserve the Gnostic heritage, but rather repressed the Christian religion completely. With the installation of a Moslem state in Egypt soon thereafter, the Gnostics all but disappeared in a historical sense.

The evidence of their existence was only recently discovered in the 1940s. Once the Nile River caves where the Gnostic manuscripts were found at Nag Hammadi and their contents deciphered, it was probable the truth would be known about the history of Christianity. The discrepancies between the versions of the Orthodox and Gnostic interpretations will be open to re-interpretation. They were diverse enough to cast doubt upon whose vision of Christian doctrine was historically accurate, the Gnostic or the Orthodox. Considering the Gnostic version had been planted in mason jars and sealed up in caves for thousands of years, while the Church's version has been modified repeatedly over the millennia since, there could be little doubt whose version has not been tampered with. It was the Gnostic one.

When the Dark Ages fell after the fall of Rome, Christian monks had total control over the Canon's contents, and no one was really paying attention to what they did with it. As the Canon had passed from hand to hand by scribes over successive Church administrations, alterations to the Canon's contents were inevitable. Furthermore it was difficult not to be biased when the overzealous had an agenda to fulfill.

Chapter 19 The Battleground Of Doctrine

In retrospect, the greatest fear of the Gnostics was that organized religion would lose the process of attaining Christ Consciousness in a bureaucracy. Hence few of the whys of the Faith would filter down to the congregation, and expedient answers would be returned for questions asked earnestly. That fear was realized with the advent of Romanized Christianity. In place of Gnosis, the Orthodox substituted education in the Sacraments, and the rules and regulations they had established.

Virtues espoused by the Christ for the purpose of instilling Love in all who fervently practiced them, were reiterated in Church doctrine but perverted in practice. The methodology of Orthodox evangelism was not conducive to the learning that was required by the process of Gnosis, but rather to brainwashing. For security's sake, ideological skyscrapers were erected to consolidate the faith in modular components, each exactly like the other. Many rules were created where a few would suffice, and a deity was fashioned to fit human needs. Piety and obedience were elevated to noble virtues, and became integral functioning parts of the Catholic faith.

To validate every move a book-God was fabricated

from the Scriptures by learned men whose concern was propagation of the faith. They breathed life into this paper-God so that it would serve the purpose for which it was invented, the domination of Man's spiritual destiny. The master plan was to baptize and dress the Christian in the clothes laid out for him, whether or not they fit. In the ensuing years, those clothes have been tailored to fit. The surrogate experience of the book-God touched all who found meaning in the words. The Catholic Church put all of its stock into the book-God because eventually it lost its feeling for the Word, and that showed in its behavior.

To equalize the faith of all members of the congregation, the Orthodox Christian educational system has stunted the growth of the gifted, while enhancing the cause of the laggard. The indoctrination of all members equally with a sanctioned version of the Canon created a middle-class spiritualist who knew enough to wet his curiosity, but not enough to quench his thirst. Many had to be satisfied with a middle-class understanding because the only Orthodox avenue to the average parishioner for knowledge was lay deaconship. To delve into the mysteries of Christhood was earmarked for a select priesthood. It was identified as a *calling*.

The priest was initially envisioned as a spiritual aspirant who sought the evolution of Christ Consciousness in himself. Since the first priests of Christendom, the apostles, were chosen by Yeshua. It followed that priests had to be called henceforth. But since the apostles took up that burden, devolution of the quality of priests has occurred. Although a few have aspired to true virtue like St Francis of Assisi, the vast majority of those who have held the title of priest have treated that position like it was only an occupation. The political and economic aspects of the job too often overshadowed the spiritual purpose of the work. The promise of a living Christ anticipated from the clergy has never fulfilled the expectation. In reality, the metaphysical rift between parishioner and priest was no greater than the distance between God and his supposed mediator, the priest. By design the priest was pronounced to be closer to God for the purposes of mediation. The parishioner was designated to develop only as far as the priest, and no further growth toward Christ Consciousness was encouraged beyond that artificial ceiling.

Because so much of Christian esoteric knowledge was withheld from the average parishioner, one had little hope of finding the answers to one's questions within the confines of one's Church. One was compelled to leave the well-charted and much-travelled mental regions for the uncharted regions of one's own mind. In this way only, could one ascend from one's designated caste. The middle-class spiritualist was granted a middle-class education, replete with gilt-edged text books, and classrooms with low ceilings.

By Orthodox faiths individuals were taught they were faulty, tempted by instincts they should deny, and burdened with duties they should not avoid. The guilt-trip laid on the individual fostered a dependence upon a savior because an erroneous assumption was made that an individual required saving. Furthermore it was presumed that the individual was incapable of saving his or her own soul. Any progress made in self-development was interrupted by the reliance upon salvation where none was really required, or even possible. From their perspective salvation was a requirement, and one was not supposed to punch his or her own ticket for it. By definition, a self-saving act was not permissible unless it was witnessed in the presence of the congregation to be validated as true, right, and effective. In other words, salvation must be sanctioned by Authority to be deemed valid.

Orthodox religions synthesized individual ideals into a

congregational identity as a mandate of God by the surrender of the individual will to the will of the congregation. Their method of synthesis could only be accomplished with the individual relinquishing his or her inalienable right of self-determination in favor of the common determination. But it meant men were determining the nature of the common good rather than God, and ordaining it to be the will of God. One may have a choice to embrace or reject their proposition, but no vote was being taken on formulating the proposition. With ideological power centered in the few, the prospects for the abuse of that power were guaranteed because the few needed that power to exercise control over the congregation, and manipulate it to do its bidding. Thus the will of the few was disguised as God's will be done and foisted upon the shoulders of a populace which did not know the difference. They willingly carried that burden until one's faith collapsed under the weight of it.

    Even if it was only for identification, many individuals still relied upon the consensus of congregation to validate their belief. Consequently a meaning for life was still sought in the documented failures of Church and State that would be exposed by an accurate interpretation of history. Throughout the Ages, the extended families of village, school, and social club have no more met the expectation, than have the mass, confession, or catechism classes provided any meaningful revelation. And that expectation was only real compassion from people rather than expediency in interpersonal relationships, an end to greed in its myriads of shapes and sizes, and the realization that Justice was not a commodity for sale. Outside of one's community support group, it was apparent that faith alone had not been the answer in affecting change in the world-at-large. The misguided sincerity of Church and State will lead to more of the same treatment if given the opportunity. And what individuals wanted most was to ground themselves in a belief that would not be washed away with the next tsunami. Thus they turned to what they believe had worked in the past to protect them from the uncertainty posed by the future. But in reality, what they needed was to listen to their hearts to determine what course to follow as the Gnostics suggested. It was certainly not a path of further servitude to the empty promises of Orthodox salvation.

Considering that what Orthodox religions promoted as spiritual learning was really no more than a mandated process of socialization, the Gnostics maintained it had little to offer in the way of enlightenment. Primarily it was used to transmit socially-acceptable principles of morality and training in the etiquette of interpersonal relationships. Because the satisfaction of human needs extended much farther than the civil authority could provide, religious authorities were instituted to foster a sense of cooperation and brotherhood between individuals. By extending the role of parental supervision, a community was formed. For the most part, Orthodox religion had assumed the role of the guardian of humanity's hopes and dreams merely because God traditionally has been named as humanity's Father in the Nicene Creed.

The spiritual orientation received in congregation has always been focused upon social rather than spiritual issues. From the earliest centuries of Church existence, the emphasis had been placed upon the necessity of moral instruction as opposed to the experience of *knowing*. Thus the ultimate aim was the refinement of human behavior. The end was clearly a societal one: namely, the making of good citizens, with the hope that an obedient citizen of civil law would also be an observer of religious doctrine and vice versa. They made observing Church law synonymous with obeying Universal Law because the perception was, they were one and the same. But it contributed very little toward establishing a spiritual frame of mind, particularly if one did not equate spirituality with religious faith.

Furthermore this educational methodology was not conducive to learning, but to resuscitation, and the formulation of religious dogma. Its ultimate success was negligible in the spiritual aspect because of the dichotomy of life and the afterlife it created. While the individual was insufficiently prepped for a material life that was in a constant state of flux, the subject of the afterlife was presented as a reward or a punishment for how one conducted one's life. Hence physical life was presented as a proving ground without a clear indication that the cause-and-effect relationship between them was the crux of the matter.

Furthermore as the history of Christianity showed the Orthodox presumed to judge those severely who were of a different opinion than they. This was one of the messages from Gnostic teachers who attempted to infuse platonic principles into the evolving Christian experience. The merger they proposed was nothing more than finding the individual intellect a place at the table for the burgeoning Christian faith. The attempt was snuffed out unceremoniously by the pious power-brokers who saw no profit in it for them. They only viewed it as a challenge to their illegitimate authority; for they viewed it as a heresy that human beings wanted to be treated like they were individuals.

Furthermore they viewed it as a challenge to the hierarchical system of authority they were attempting to institute whereby an individual would always be ruled by corporal authority standing in for a heavenly authority, as a king ruled over his subjects. Their perverted interpretation of the principle of *as above, so below,* envisioned an earthly king fully-vested in administrating the dictates of his heavenly power; as if by some stretch of the imagination, they rationalized humanity was in desperate need of a ruling body.

The Gnostics maintained that good and evil were the inventions of religious doctrine, concocted by the purveyors of said doctrine to enable the faithful to view the world and everything in it as black or white, contrary to the scientific observation that everything really had color. Living color made it account for a wondrous diversity of opinion radiant in shades of difference. But the precise objective of doctrine was to transform the difficult choices of life into easy, manageable ones because what Orthodox religion was really all about was managing the thought processes of its chosen congregation. No freethinking individual could tolerate the ideological demands of religious doctrine because it was contrary to the doctrine of free will which served as a counterpoint to its dictums espoused by moralistic, tyrannical regimes. These regimes have specialized in deluding the congregation into believing it truly had made a choice.

Supposedly one of the philosophical pillars of the Orthodox faith was the unlimited application of free will. Ironically this seemed strangely out of place within the context of any expression of faith which placed an accent upon the strict observance of God's will. While one had the ability to choose right over wrong, the inherent aim of tribal faith was to ensure the correct choice was made consistently. Entering an age that put a premium on intellectual self-sufficiency, it was the essence of this contradiction that consigned Orthodox faith to extinction within the educated strata of humanity.

Many parishioners had been disappointed by the outcome of their most earnest prayers to an invisible God even though they believed they were exercising the tenets of their Orthodox faith in good conscience. Many have grown impatient of waiting for HIM to reveal HIMSELF in their daily lives in the manner they had chosen, instead of the manner in which IT chose. Thus they swore allegiance to a God of literature who they imagined could deliver a more tangible reward. However earnestly they may have sought spiritual fulfillment from a God of their own invention, intellectual and emotional satisfaction was received instead. As a consequence, a life of comfort and happiness had become more highly prized than a life of pure intent. As long as expectations were met, it would always remain the same.

However once the Orthodox faithful developed a habit of praying for material things, they lost prospective on the meaning of spirituality. Consumed by a life of materialistic intent, they could not conceive of the virtue inherent in a selfless motive. Thus these desires tarnished the stated altruistic aims of humanitarian principles of the Orthodoxy, ultimately the prognosis being, a moral challenge to the belief system. All too often, however, they failed to recognize it. The faith of the Orthodox was focused upon achieving an elusive salvation through sanctioned means without realizing the salvation they sought was only achieved through a purity of heart, like the Gnostics had always maintained. There existed no silver bullet to kill the demon that poisoned the mind.

Notwithstanding sectarian leanings, no amount of

soothing a bruised ego will erase the ill will one may harbor for the injustices they had suffered. No compensation was enough reparation for the pain endured by all in the lapse of brotherhood. In the truest sense, every noble human virtue radiated naturally from a pureness of heart. There were no other means at one's disposal to avoid the prospect of being set adrift in the doldrums where no fair wind could substitute for a lack of compassion. There existed no magic potion or secret doctrine in which to believe that permitted one to lift the veil from one's eyes. There was a far simpler explanation than the convoluted doctrines the Orthodox faith proposed to validate what one's reasonable course of action should be. In the final analysis, sectarianism just revealed itself to be a wedge to drive people further apart.

Unfortunately critical thinking on this proposition was obscured by the cloud enveloping the Orthodox faith. It was the final refuge for those who did not wish to acknowledge the element of doubt that may persist in their own minds. Hence, they chose to believe all of what was imparted and deny none of it. And more importantly they questioned neither the veracity of what was written, nor its source; for they were assured beyond a reasonable doubt it was God by a reputable authority who claimed to HIS spokesman.

Furthermore it was the individual who interpreted it who made the claim, not an impartial auditor by any stretch of the imagination. Unfortunately their chosen book was an inanimate object and could not be interrogated. The faithful had witnessed none of it, but yet they believed. Their confidence was bolstered by a gospel verse chiding the apostle Thomas (as if it was planted for that purpose) when he insisted upon viewing the marks of the crucifixion: *"Jesus saith unto him, because you have seen me, you have believed; blessed are those who have not seen but yet have believed" (John 20: 28-29).*

Truly the believers were the most knowledgeable of individuals or the most gullible. It depended upon one's perspective. No one could state with absolute certainty which was true, nor would the truly righteous even try. Instead throughout the millennia Thomas had been labeled as the Doubter and criticized for his apparent infidelity. A rational individual would say Thomas was asking the right question at the right time. He required proof to be a true believer, and from his vantage point that would be defined as one who took care not to delude himself. Thus it may be interpreted as a lesson for the ages rather than a scolding from the Master.

The agony of Orthodox faith lies in the acceptance of

doctrine and ideology even when it was discovered that it conflicted with the Truth. The Truth one knew within oneself and never spoke to others was the Truth that never changes. It was the Truth that could not be put into words. The truth one shouted from the rooftops was not the truth that endured. That Truth was the one exhaled with each breath. The ecstasy of Gnostic faith was the preponderance of right thinking and right doing, whereas its agony consisted of the opposite. Right thinking and doing was symbolized in a biblical statement, *"Thou shalt also decree a thing, and it shall be established unto thee, and light shall shine upon thy ways" (Job 22:28)*. Therefore salvation through faith was entirely in each individual's hands. It was not a prerogative of doctrine or ideology no matter how hard an ideology wanted to make it one to validate its existence.

The Orthodox used their educational strategy to produce a consistent and homogenous brand of Christianity that was uniformly practiced. The non-conformist individual could not be tolerated in any stitch because it disturbed the thought tidy pattern they wove. The classroom of Christianity was designed to produce knowledgeable, obedient, Christian citizens, and had no place reserved for the difficult inquirer. Ordinary men and women were not informed that Christhood was a consciousness that could be attained. The Gnostics had figured this out by observing the methods and practices of the Essene, and that assumption was confirmed in the base content of the Gnostic gospels. The congregation was taught to obey a self-legitimizing authority that legislated its own laws. The transmutation of the dense into the fine substance, a metamorphosis of soul that the Christ previewed on the screen of life was the way it offered to humanity. Never once did he claim it was his possession but instead a birthright that could be exercised by anyone. His life was an attempt to prove its viability. And it was the essential point of his existence that the Orthodox chose to ignore in their formula.

Chapter 20 The Legacy Of The Media Merchants

In purging Christianity of all Gnostic tendencies, the Orthodox strengthened the mandate of the Universal Church. With their competition formally eradicated, the Universal Church remained as the sole remnant of official Christianity. For their steadfast refusal to submit to Orthodox authority, the Gnostics were disenfranchised with extreme prejudice. Their extinction was planned and executed like a military operation by those who desired a monopoly in their market.

After centuries of modifications to the original faith, the Roman Catholic Church bears only a familial resemblance to the Christine church of James, its Palestinian forbearer. Retaining only the mainline teachings of Yeshua the Christ, numerous rules and regulations were instituted to solidify the position of the Church in the Society of Man. In burdening humanity with a dogmatic rendition of the Synoptic gospels instead of attending to the spiritual needs of the people, Church fathers displayed a love of congregation, not a love of Man. Rather than showing the parishioner the potential for spiritual ascension, the Church collected tithes to spend on gaudy costumes for its grand ceremonies. The parishioner was granted license to worship but not to grow. He or she was ever to remain static in his or her allegiance and obligation to the Universal Church. In serving itself, the Church imagined it was serving God and Man.

In place of Gnosis, the Orthodox substituted indoctrination, its form of education. To equalize the knowledge of all members of the congregation, the Orthodox Christian system stunted the growth of the gifted. While the Orthodox claimed the ornate trappings of pomp and ceremony revealed the innate desire to give God the best of everything one had to offer, it really was a prodigious display of materialism substituting one Golden Calf for another. Their reasoning was materialism at its best was what God deserved. Hence the spiritual focus of the Universal Church was blurred with material concerns from the start. While it was not inherently wrong to devote your works to God, the obsessive desires of religious bigotry and intolerance crept into the intense fervor of the once-righteous, despoiling it. Never was one wrong until one was convinced one was always right beyond the shadow of a doubt.

The Gnostic subculture had been viewed as a threat because of its stubborn insistence upon a leadership based upon Virtue. Because of its supermarket-mentality the

Gnostics viewed the Catholic Church as a cheap imitation of the pure principles of peace, love and understanding in which they claimed belief. Detesting the side-show mentality of pomp and ceremony in the celebration of the mass, the Gnostics likened it to the moneychangers in the temple. They further enraged the Orthodox by suggesting that the next Coming of the Christ would result in a second expulsion from the temple. But this time it would be the Orthodox that would be expelled.

The Gnostics were proclaimed heretics because of a refusal to recognize an authoritarian bureaucracy as their Church. The Orthodox was viewed as predisposing a rule by Divine Right, an assumption made they were the foundation upon which it was built. They canonized a collection of books they had rewritten, seeing in it what they wished. It was not so much what the Gnostics believed as it was their antagonism toward serialization and classification that fueled the ire of the Orthodox bishops. What they perceived as a smug self-righteous attitude on the Gnostic side was evidence of their self-confidence in the truth of their faith. Significantly it was the Orthodox that slew the Gnostic like Cain slew Abel, polarizing men again, but this time the issue was free speech, not jealousy. With this genocide, the promise of human reconciliation offered by the Christ would seem to be spurned in favor of religious bigotry.

The Catholic Church did not rely upon the Christ for inspiration despite the feigned piety. Instead they manipulated the facts to produce the desired response from the congregation because theirs was an interest in corporal dominion, not eternal life. The negativity sown in the pursuit of noble causes like the Crusades had made bitter enemies among unnatural foes. In the name of God, many wars had been authenticated despite the commandment forbidding murder under any circumstances. In many instances, the Church had ignored Universal Law, and rationalized it as with the best of intentions. In the process, faith in God became faith in the Church among its constituents. One could not express a faith in God and be considered virtuous without Church affiliation. When in actuality, there was no spiritual connection.

With knowledge of the Scriptures came a share in salvation. Hence all Hindus, Moslems, Jews, Buddhists, and pagans were sentenced to an existence of ignorant heathenism in the estimation of Church authority. In their defense, the heathens often returned the favor. An intense egocentrism of religious preeminence enveloped the catholic movement that resulted in righteous crusades and violent persecutions to cleanse humanity by force if necessary. In the Church's defense, the Muslims did the same. But two wrongs did not make a right. The history of Catholicism has fulfilled its mandate, revealing an attitude of religious fascism that discredited any declared altruistic motive. The Spanish Inquisition was the supreme example of religious intolerance and Christo-Fascism. Throughout its reign, the Universal Church has been controlled by a small group of men who professed an understanding of the teachings of Yeshua the Christ as if that was his surname instead of a title. However that belief was proof they did not grasp the meaning of the Christ designation.

In forecasting the false hope of salvation for those who made no effort, but only belonged, a grave injustice has been done to the spirit of Man. Choosing to bury its talent in the hard Earth the Catholic Church never reflected the Spirit of the Faith, or the love of the Son. Wealth, power, and manifest destiny have warped the message of peace, love, and brotherhood delivered by the apostles, and caused the Church to covet the place of God instead. With an obedient humanity yoked to the plow of Christendom, the neat furrows of Christian mediocrity produced a bountiful harvest of stunted growths. During the period of Church reign, the search for Truth stalled because they believed it had been found. Few were motivated to look further. Using fear of castigation and excommunication, the Church had managed to the limit the growth options available to the inquiring mind. Intellectual and moral subjugation have adversely affected the growth of the human individual, thereby leaving him book-wise and life-foolish.

The institutionalization of Christianity has altered the course of Western Civilization forever, and elevated or corrupted it depending upon the viewpoint taken. Many had been misled by the self-appointed shepherds of Christendom. During eras fraught with civil and religious strife, the ruthless held sway. At the point of a sword, the faith was spread. Authority manipulated the weak-minded with self-fulfilling prophecies and pastoral lies, while stripping them of their personal dignity. The debasement of the human spirit was offered in the guise of Penance, and from his knees Man learned to be humble. However, the object of that humility was not God, nor the Christ, but rather the Universal Church.

The sanctity of all life and social justice for all were not issues of universal concern. They were limited to the scope of the congregation. The truly righteous have only had those concerns for all men because their thoughts were pure. The profane, on the other hand, had no such concern at any time. They denied purity with their actions and revealed their actual purpose which was the preservation of ideological and social dominance. Hence revelations of the origins of historic Christianity will ultimately lead humanity to the Truth; for it was at this time sequence that the West first encountered a realized master and rejected him.

Once Europe began to emerge from the Dark Ages, men were inspired to think again, and their thoughts spawned a rebellion against the Universal Church. Renaissance thinkers like Martin Luther and St Thomas Aquinas questioned the substance of its teachings and right of its authoritarianism. Those of the faithful, who had had enough tongue-lashing, confessional-wisdom, and reward and punishment, stretched their wings. The imaginations of heaven and hell were losing their grip on the fears of the populace. The Orthodox fanatics conducted inquisitions in several European countries in an effort to still free thought. But the ultimate success of these inquisitions was to spark the Renaissance to greater heights of involvement as did the Roman persecutions.

When the Renaissance flourished, the Renaissance man sought Truth anew. He began to question and the answers he found not in his Church. The end of feudalism had signaled a decline of authority for the Catholic Church as well. The stagnancy of the feudal mentality gave way to a rebirth of intellectual and spiritual curiosity. With the advent of individualism, free will became the cause for the Renaissance man, and liberty originated in casting off the yoke of the church-dominated mind. As the human being, stepped out of his feudal role, he began to realize his potential. The Truth has always been available to the inquiring mind. All that has ever been required was the seeking.

Divorced from the realm of scientific fact, the fathers of the Church toiled in a twilight realm where piety reigned supreme. In such a frame of mind, the pious Christian could justify a belief that the Earth was flat because by casual observation it appeared to be. In the time of Aristophanes circa 300 BCE, Euclid, a pagan Egyptian, invented a value called PI which was used to calculate the circumference of round objects, the pious adhered to an erroneous belief. As every school child knows, flat surfaces were measured in linear units. They had no depth. One may draw one's own conclusion.

Pythagoras who lived several centuries before the birth of the Christ had already proposed the notion that the Earth was spherical in shape if for no other reason than a sphere was representative of perfect form. Aristotle echoed this belief, and the revival of classical study in Europe brought his ideas to the forefront again by St. Thomas Aquinas, among others. In 1492 CE, Columbus proved the pagans to be correct in their assertions.

Secondly, Church officials endorsed the notion that the Earth was roughly 6000 years old because by calculating the lineages of all of the patriarchs in Genesis and adding the time that had ensued since the Bible was written, it approximated that total. Since the human being was pronounced to be a direct descendant of God by the Nicene Creed, such a calculation was deemed appropriate. It mattered not to the pious men of the day that using the Bible to calculate the age of the Earth was a violation of every known principle of logic known to the Greeks, Romans, Persians, or Babylonians. In this instance, the application of logic was irrelevant because the source of the information was sacrosanct. Without a means to refute it, the unbelief stood unchallenged. Modern Science now estimated the Earth was approximately 4.35 billion years old, and the Universe was approximately 14.7 billion years old. With subsequent scientific advancements these numbers tend to vary slightly, but they are not ever repudiated.

Thirdly, pious men accepted the belief the Earth sat at the center of the universe, reasoning it must because the human being was the centerpiece of God's Creation. It did not occur to the pious men of yesteryear that the universe could have existed for any other purpose than to provide lodging for God's so-called chosen creation. Evidently the pious were not capable of thinking in anything but ethnocentric terms. When Copernicus dared to propose the theory of a heliocentric solar system, he was excommunicated from the Church, and castigated by medieval society. To save himself from eternal damnation because he was a pious Christian, he recanted his heliocentric theory on his deathbed. He was exonerated during the Renaissance, but he died in disgrace because too many were comfortable in their institutional ignorance. Even educated pagans held the identical belief but no one was persecuted because they adopted a differing opinion.

Only in the twilight realm of faith could such arbitrary gross miscalculations go unchallenged for hundreds of years, primarily because the pretentious men of faith intentionally discarded a prodigious legacy of pagan science and cosmology. Merely because the ideas were the product of pagan cultures, they were discarded out-of-hand. Until Christians came of age during the Renaissance and began to question the choices of the Universal Church, they could not have conceived how wrong they had been. And it begged the question why the beliefs of the theologians of the day would be right, if they were so wrong about the world in which they lived. Would then their treasured intimations be wrong about the God who created it or HIS son?

Chapter 21 Christ, The Traveler

The so-called lost years of Jesus, from ages 12 to 30, were not really lost because the Christ knew where he was. His whereabouts were unknown to the chroniclers of his words and deeds in the Universal Church who did not know the man, or how he came to be the Christ. One of the messages of this book was: Yeshua was not born the Christ. He evolved into that status with the help of the Essene, and that opportunity was open to any and all human beings. Even though an individual might not achieve it, the opportunity was offered. The underlying message of his journey of self-discovery was to illuminate the path one would travel, and dealing with the trials and travails one would have to endure to achieve Christ Consciousness. Quite frankly what really mattered was what was actually achievable in real terms.

In time, what also became clear was that the one individual who everyone professed belief in, namely Jesus of Nazareth had gaping holes in his life story. It was the height of irony that the individual a person of faith should know everything about was probably the one who he or she really knew the least about. From the ages of 12 to 30, it was assumed by authorities of the Universal Church, Jesus of

Nazareth led a nondescript life as a carpenter in Nazareth for that period of time. On the other hand, THE AQUARIAN GOSPEL OF JESUS THE CHRIST made the bold claim that he had spent 18 years traveling the known world on a quest for knowledge. Therefore either little was apparently known about him, or there was a systematic effort to cover it up. Both assertions could not be true. Was it possible such a massive cover up could have been perpetuated for all of these years, and for what reason?

The silence had been deafening concerning this period until the 20th Century. With the publication of Nicholas Roerich's travel log, his discoveries in India during the years, 1925 through 1928, were made public. One of these discoveries came from examinations of ancient Hindu scrolls, reportedly from the Vedas, which named a St Issa as a visitor from the West who lived at the time of Yeshua and Apollonius of Tyana. *St Issa* performed amazing feats of what the Hindus referred to as *moving the prana*. Many have interpreted St Issa to have been the historical Yeshua who visited India prior to beginning his ministry in Judea. According to Roerich's travel log, St Issa sought the council of the philosophers and spiritual masters of his day. As was suggested earlier in this text, the most logical candidate to be the legendary St Issa was not Yeshua, but instead was Apollonius of Tyana. For all intents and purposes, the latter appeared to be the logical choice. It was this author's belief that the attempt to hang the St Issa label on Jesus of Nazareth was an attempt by some to explain how he became the Christ.

> *He passed his [St Issa] time in several ancient cities of India such as Benares. All loved him because Issa dwelt in peace with Vaishyas and Shudras whom he instructed and helped. But the Brahmins and Kshatriyas told him that Brahma forbade those to approach who were created out of his womb and feet.The Vaishyas were allowed to listen to the Vedas only on Holidays and the Shudras were forbidden not only to be Present at the reading of the Vedas, but could not even look at them. Issa said that man had filled the temples with his abominations. In order to pay homage to metal and stones, man sacrificed his fellows in whom dwells a spark of Supreme Spirit. Man demeans those who labor by the sweat of their brows, in order to gain the good will of the sluggard who sits at the lavishly set board. But they who deprive their brothers of the common blessing shall be stripped of it. Vaishyas and Shudras were struck with astonishment and asked what they could perform. Issa bade them "Worship not the idols. Do not consider yourself first. Do not humiliate your neighbor. Help the poor. Sustain the feeble. Do evil to no one. Do not covet that which is possessed by others." Many, learning of such words, decided to kill I ssa. But Issa, forewarned, departed from this place by night. Afterward Issa went to Nepal and into the Himalayan Mountains "well, perform for us a miracle," demanded the servers of the Temple. Then Issa replied*

to them: "Miracles made their appearance from the very day when the world was created. He who cannot behold them is deprived of the greatest gift of life. But woe to you, enemies of men, woe unto you, if you await that it should attest his power by miracle." "Issa" taught that men should not strive to behold the Eternal Spirit with one's own eyes but feel it with his heart, and to become a pure and worthy soul. "Not only shall you not make human offerings, but you Must not slaughter animals, because all is given for the use of man. Do not steal the goods of others, because that would be usurpation from your near one. Do not cheat, that you may in turn not be cheated.... Beware, ye, who divert men from the true path and who fill the people with superstitions and prejudices, who blind the vision of the seeing ones, and who preach subservience to material things."

An 18th Century apocalyptic text, THE AQUARIAN GOSPEL OF JESUS THE CHRIST, chronicled St Issa's 18 years of world travel from Hierapolis, Egypt to the foothills of the Himalayas. It was published in 1908. It reported that he visited many countries including Egypt, Greece, Persia, and India in the pursuit of Truth. In each locale, he conferred with the masters and teachers of his day. Some consultations were conducted in the flesh, others perhaps with a master in their ascended state in Spirit. The author, Levi H. Dowling, claimed to have transcribed the book as received from the Akashic record. One may consider that casted doubt upon its authenticity, but that depended upon the nature of one's faith. When paired with Roerich's travel log and the journals of other adventurers of his day who made the trek in that direction, the details compared favorably. Also the details presented compared favorably with the teachings of the savior as presented in the Nag Hammadi gospels. Of course the Gnostic gospels had not been discovered in the 1920s so neither Roerich nor Dowling could have reviewed them, and compared notes. Neither was much of anything known about the Essene at the time.

To the contrary, Orthodox tradition circulated the explanation that the lost years of Jesus was a hoax because the Christ was living the simple life of a carpenter preparing for his ministry. His life was deemed to be as nondescript as any Hebrew peasant of the time, and the reason given for not mentioning it in the Scriptures was because there was nothing worth mentioning. This seemed a logical explanation for the uniformed of that time. However one must wonder why such a critical, formative period in any human being's life was declared inconsequential in any official capacity. The inconsistency of promoting a Messiah image without having the facts to back it up was baffling. It seemed the Orthodox took the son of God reputation a bit far.

Seemingly the difference in Orthodox and Gnostic

views of the man and the Messiah could be chalked up to seeing the Christ as he was as opposed to what he became. The inconsistency of perception exhibited by Orthodox and Gnostic in how they each viewed the Christ as a man and as a deity, resulted in eventual conflict. The psychology of the Messiah complex in both traditions was rooted in fundamentally diverse attitudes. The Orthodox perceived the Christ as a mystery, while the Gnostics saw the Christ as the end-result of a development process.

Though it was not historically documented, some Gnostic sects could have been aware of the events comprising the 18 lost years. That may be the reason for their uncompromising stance on the Monophysite versus the Dyophysite nature of the Christ/Man. In essence, a reason was provided for the Orthodox mystery position. Supposedly the Christ's abilities in moving pranic energy (his miracles) became more believable in this context. If he had learned the procedures from Hindu mystics and Classical sources, it provided a reason for his accomplishments at 30 years of age. His journeys revealed him to be a man of knowledge who investigated and experimented who proved to himself there was a reason to believe. He expressed the truths he learned at every opportunity in his sermons as well as his works. The inability of those who witnessed his words and deeds truly reflected their limitation of insight or Gnosis.

Since the Fathers of the Universal Church were so meticulous in their formulation of the Canon, the question of the lost 18 years would surely have arisen. The apparent resolution was an official policy declaring that the Christ spent ages 12 through 30 in Nazareth learning the carpentry trade. It was deemed to be years of no consequence. But how could a man exhibiting such talent live a life of no consequence? It has been a glaring inconsistency in the psychology of the Messiah because a revelation of his travels lent credence to his Messiah image.

But perhaps it seemed inconsistent because the Christ was not the Messiah of all who claimed him. He was the Messiah, aka The Teacher of Righteousness, prophesied and awaited by the Essene, the lost tribe which produced all of the other Hebrew prophets. Yeshua, the Teacher of Righteousness, was the last of their number. At regular intervals, a Jewish prophet would emerge from the desert to scold the Hebrews. Their works were recorded in books the Essene kept. The Essene may have not considered the Pharisees or Sadducees, the corporate intelligentsia of their day, worthy of having a Messiah. But the Essene role and responsibility was to be the Sheppard to the flock until the Teacher of Righteousness appeared in accordance with their prophecy.

Yeshua, however, was more compassionate than some of his more judgmental brothers and sisters in the Essene desert tribe who were noted for their sectarianism. He promoted a non-sectarian view of Love, Peace and Brotherhood that was more in line with the teachings of THE CHILDREN OF THE LAW OF ONE. The Church fathers interpreted that view in a sectarian way, as within the confines of the Universal Church, or body of Christ. Hence Yeshua's ideas did not appeal to the religious or secular authorities of his time, unless they could be used to control multitudes.

Lack of knowledge and understanding of Christhood on the part of the Orthodox has caused a fundamental misunderstanding of the Christ and the man, Yeshua. They each came to be synonymous and used interchangeably. The distinction between them was obscured as a matter of convenience. This showed in how Christ was appended to the name of Yeshua like it was his surname. In the final analysis, Christ was no person's surname and that was the point. It was a title that one earned, an achievement like Bishop or Rabbi. It was not just a state of being, but the end-result of a process. And if one did not understand that distinction, one could not understand how the status was achieved.

Furthermore THE AQUARIAN GOSPEL OF JESUS THE CHRIST described in detail how and why the Christ could have achieved Christhood, even though Yeshua received his training in Egypt. Supposedly before the journey around the known world began, Yeshua and John the Baptist who was his cousin received their early education in Egypt. The importance of this education was paramount to knowing how to communicate with Yahweh which was also one's higher self. In essence, prayer and meditation represented that communication with Yahweh. Specifically it was that part of oneself that was connected to Yahweh. In THE AQUARIAN GOSPEL OF JESUS THE CHRIST, Salome, an Essene teacher, who instructed the families of Yeshua and John the Harbinger, as he was called in that text, for several years in Egypt, provided an apt description of what prayer was. She said.

> "Yahweh speaks to hearts apart; and hearts apart just speak to him; and this is prayer. It is not prayer to shout at Yahweh, to stand, or sit, or kneel and tell him all about the sins of men. It is not prayer to tell the Holy One how great HE is, how good HE is how strong, and how compassionate. Yahweh is not man

to be brought up by praise of man. Prayer is the ardent wish that every way of life be light; that every act be crowned with good; that every living thing be prospered by our ministry. A noble deed, a helpful word is prayer; a fervent, an effectual prayer. By thought, not words, the heart is blest, then let us pray." They prayed, but not a word was said; but in that holy silence every heart was blest.

In addition to learning how to communicate with Yahweh so his thoughts would be cleansed, Yeshua also was instructed upon how to communicate with men. That communication included an insight into forms of love. To embody love one had to intuitively know all forms of love. In the Greek culture, those forms were Eros, meaning sexual love, Philia, meaning brotherly love, Storge meaning familial or parental affection, and Agape meaning universal love or compassion for one's fellow man. The purpose of this instruction was to provide men with the insight upon how to communicate with each other. In order to preach a way to live, one must first understand all of the meanings and expressions of love before one could be entrusted to show the way to a more perfect union.

It was thought the greatest form of communion between human beings was that between a man and a woman. That was the perfect union of masculine and feminine divine principles that produced life. Since the union of man and woman engendered life itself on the physical plane, the merger of process and principle was paramount to success of the race itself. A harmonious union of man and woman produced well-balanced offspring. In the Sermon on the Mount as detailed in THE AQUARIAN GOSPEL OF JESUS THE CHRIST, Yeshua described that perfect union.

> *The law forbids adultery; but in the eyes of the law adultery is an overt act, the satisfaction of the sensuous self outside the marriage bonds. Now marriage in the sight of law is a promise made by man and woman, by the sanction of a priest, to live forever in harmony and love. No priest or officer has the power from God to bind two souls in wedded love. What is the marriage tie? Is it comprised in what a priest or officer may say? Is it the scroll on which the officer or priest has written the permission for the two that they will love each other until death? Is love a passion that is subject to the will of man? Can man pick up his love, as it would pick up precious gems, and lay it down, or give it out to any one? Can love be bought and sold like sheep? Love is the power of God that binds two souls and makes them one; there is no power on Earth that can dissolve the bond. The bodies may be forced apart by man or death for just a little; but they will meet again. Now, in this bond of God we find the marriage tie; all other unions are but bonds of straw, and they who live in them commit adultery. The same as they who satisfy their lust without the sanction of an officer or priest. But more than this; one man or woman who indulges lustful thoughts commits adultery. Whom God has joined together man can part; whom man has joined together live in sin.*

Finally to solidify his understanding of the mission, he was embarking upon, St Issa was provided instruction on the requirements of the New Age to imbue him with a sense of purpose. The coming age referred to by Vidyapati was the Age of Pisces. The New Age that was alluded to was the Age of Aquarius. That instruction was provided by Vidyapati, the Hindu sage of the Piscean Age. In the conversation with Vidyapati as detailed in THE AQUARIAN GOSPEL OF JESUS THE CHRIST, the requirements of the Piscean and Aquarian Ages were described.

> *And St Issa said, "Our God must loathe the tinseled show of priests and priestly things. When men array themselves in showy garbs to indicate that they are servants of the Gods, and strut like gaudy birds to be admired by men, because of piety or any other thing, the Holy One must turn away in sheer disgust. All the people are alike the servants of our Father-God, are kings and priests. Will not the coming age demand complete destruction of the priestly caste, as well as every other caste and inequality among sons of men?" And Vidyapati said, "The coming age [Piscean] is not the age of spirit life and men will pride them selves in wearing priestly robes, and chanting pious chants to dvertise themselves as saints. The simple rites you will introduce will be extolled by those who follow you, until the sacred service of the age will far outshine in gorgeousness the priestly service of the Brahmic age. This is a problem men must solve. The perfect \ age [Aquarian] will come when every man will be a priest and men will not array themselves in special garb to advertise their piety."*

To reaffirm the message St Issa had received from Vidyapati concerning the requirements of the Ages, he was given a message when he visited the Oracle at Delphi in Greece. The net effect of that message confirmed that he had become the living oracle. The Christ consciousness had been brought forth within him.

> *And when Apollo stood before the Oracle he spoke and said, "Apollo, sage of Greece, the bell strikes twelve, the midnight of the ages now has come. With in the womb of Nature ages are conceived. They gestate and are born in glory with the rising sun, and when the ageic sun goes down and the age disintegrates and dies. The Delphic Age has been an age of glory and renown. The Gods have spoken to the sons of men through oracles of wood, and gold, and precious stones. The Delphic sun has set. The Oracle will go into decline. the time is near when men will hear its voice no more. The Gods will speak to man by man. The living Oracle now stands within these sacred groves; The Logos from on high has come. From henceforth will decrease my wisdom and power; from henceforth will increase the wisdom andthe power of him, Immanuel. Let all the masters stay; let every creature hear and honour him, Immanuel. "And then the Oracle spoke not again for forty days, And the priests and the people were amazed. They came from near and far to hear the Living Oracle speak forth the wisdom of the Gods. And Jesus and the Grecian sage returned, and in Apollo's home, the Living Oracle spoke forth for forty days.*

St Issa received this message on his return journey home. It represented the culmination of his journey and the purpose for it; the reason being, the knowledge he had received over the course of his journey had jelled. This was an indication he had become the Christ. In essence it meant he had evolved to that status despite the fact that the Orthodox had always claimed that he was born the Christ. But of course if St Issa had been Yeshua, he would have not had to leave Egypt to achieve Christhood. Therefore it was clear the entire purpose of this journey was to confirm the ascension to Christhood for Jesus of Nazareth. Centuries after the fact, the Orthodox had their justification to bestow on a humble carpenter from Nazareth, the title of the Christ, even though it was unnecessary.

Chapter 22 THE MISSION OF YESHUA THE CHRIST

The Essene prophet, Yeshua the Christ, was able to envision that tribal religion would be humanity's undoing. In his teachings, he attempted to show humanity an alternative. His teachings touched upon the efficacy of Virtue, Compassion and Understanding, rather than Piety and Obedience. How Universal Law worked at its deepest level and how humanity fit into the grand scheme of things were his issues of concern, rather than how his relative doctrines persevered. He never wrote his teachings down nor instructed his followers to pen doctrines. Through an oral tradition, he endeavored to write directly into the human heart. His teachings taught an individual how to evolve in his or her thinking from a tribal to a universal view through an understanding of the principles of Natural Law. For an individual to reach his or her highest and greatest good, it was a necessary step. If an individual was to reach that end, one would only do it through the means the prophet taught.

The dilution of his teachings led to the perversion of the process. Suffice it to say, the true focus of an individual's spiritual empowerment recognized no ideological bias or fulfillment of messianic vested interest. It was the net effect of the natural gravitational pull toward the Light. One needed only to react to the cause that enabled it, and step into the Light. The inertia would be sufficient to pull one into alignment, once one had begun moving in the right direction.

There was a reason why Yeshua never wrote his teachings down. It was not because he was illiterate. Yeshua wanted people to carry his teachings in their hearts. Writing them down provided an opportunity to pervert them. It enabled one to interject one's own likes and dislikes into the mix. If people had direct access to their feelings, however, they could not be perverted unless of course they wished to circumvent those feelings themselves. His faith was a living faith.

A case in point was The Sermon on the Mount. It was the crowning achievement of his ministry. It was the core of his mission. The Beatitudes were an encapsulated version of what it meant to be his follower. It was a collection of spiritual and moral principles, primarily peace, love and the brotherhood of Man, which were the focal point of his teaching. Yeshua spoke the words and his disciples wrote it down for posterity. The event itself was incorporated into what was acknowledged now to be part of Scripture, the life and times of Yeshua the Christ.

If Yeshua could read Scripture, a reasonable assumption was that he could write it as well. He was a rabbi. If not officially, then within the context of its meaning to the first century Jew, he met the definition. To his disciples, he was a teacher and counselor in every sense of the word. His teachings were simple enough to be remembered without too much effort. They were clear and precise. Even his parables could be grasped quite easily by the dullest among the populace. They were made simple enough to avoid misinterpretation. Those who did not get it did not want to get it. They had their own agenda to fulfill, and it was to subvert his teaching. His adversaries did so because it threatened the social and economic standing and ideological preeminence of the rich and the powerful. The Pharisees, Sadducees, and Roman bureaucrats were good examples of those who denied the teachings of the Christ. These naysayers were similar to the Evangelicals and conservative politicians of the present day. They each had their own agendas to fulfill, and those agendas were not designed to promote love, peace, and the brotherhood of Man to be sure. It was their own particular version of the prosperity gospel. One they could literally bank on to stuff their pockets.

If the Christ, the personification of love and

quintessential proponent of secular humanism of all time, could not turn the Sanhedrin and the Roman Empire from their corrupt ways in his day, rest assured no one else was capable of doing it. They did it by choice. They had him crucified anyway. If he could have spared himself a horrific death on the cross, he would have. However he knew in his heart of hearts he was consigned to an untimely end because he dared to speak the Truth to those who felt threatened by it. He dared to speak Truth to power, and he paid the ultimate price for it. Even if he could have convinced them of their error, they would not dare to accept it. His teachings endangered the Sanhedrin's stranglehold on the intellectual, spiritual, and ethical commerce of their particular brand of tribal faith. When the Romans put a stranglehold on the intellectual commerce of the known world, it solidified their Empire. Throughout history, Yeshua's fate was the fate of truth tellers who ran afoul of the keepers of the shell game staged by the tribal authorities.

Take heed from the lesson the death of the Christ offered, and understand that the penalty for challenging tribal authority bore a price few were understandably unwilling to pay. His unintended sacrifice was compounded by the misguided proposition that this man died to atone for the sins of humanity. Could a rational individual be assured that the death of one man provided another with life everlasting? If and when one understood the content of Spiritual Law or the purpose of karmic debt, one realized this was not a plausible explanation for the essence of one's life or the consequences of one's death. Moreover it was an erroneous assumption that one's errors could ever be resolved by one other than the one who committed them as the Gnostics, Essene, and Great White Brotherhood contended all along.

    The mission of the Christ was to re-institute balance in the human condition. The ages-old supposition that the Christ was sent on a mission to permit himself to be crucified to accomplish the salvation of humanity was patently erroneous. Such a belief was beyond the pale of reasonable doubt. No human being, even if he could be acclaimed the son of God, wielded that kind of power. That belief ran counter to the law of cause and effect. Furthermore in the Canonical gospels as well as the Gnostic gospels, the Christ repeatedly referred to himself as the son of man. Never did he refer to himself as the son of God. That crucifixion-resurrection-of-the-son-of-God fiction was concocted years afterward by those despairing in his death whose primary concern was with their own survival under the shadow of the iron eagle of pagan Rome. Moreover the Universal Church had a vested interest in covering their tracks by putting the words in his mouth to make it seem as if he had planned a human sacrifice, that being his crucifixion and resurrection. They made it fit neatly into a scheme of intentional sacrifice and estimated salvation. In actuality, the Christ did nothing more than resign himself to that fate. He allowed Nature to take its course, lest he wished to undo the good work he had done.

In addition, a proposition was invented for those seeking a justification for their belief the majority of his followers found to be insufficient in the thoughts, words, and deeds of the consummate humanist. That proposition was: if the Christ would willingly die for his beliefs, how true and potent was his cause? Their reasoning followed that: who was greater than one who sacrificed his life for his cause? Did his sacrifice not justify a constituency? Then if he rose from the dead three days later after he predicted it, did he not prove that he was the son of God? This was the essence of their self-fulfilling prophecy. Hence the glorification of the resurrection proved to be the focal point they needed.

Thereafter this sacrifice eclipsed his life's work which was to preach love, peace and the brotherhood of Man.

Whether or not the resurrection was his intention, it served the grand illusion that one may possess a get-out-of-jail-free card if he or she be a true believer. In reality that free pass never existed. The task was to come to terms with one's errors, and atone for them. In other words, balance one's personal ledger, the Jewish practice of atonement. That was the only explanation which did not fly in the face of the law of cause and effect, one of the cornerstones of Natural Law. This belief had been a cornerstone of Hindu and Buddhist faith for time immemorial. It only made sense that it applied to the human condition regardless of Faith.

Whereas the Law of Moses was originally designated to be the tribal guidelines for the twelve tribes of Israel, the teachings of the Christ, aka The Teacher of Righteousness, were designated for all of humanity. They were intended to cut across tribal lines. Thus his attempt to preach love and forgiveness to all of humanity, notwithstanding tribal affiliation or national origin, was for the highest and noblest purpose imaginable. It put him into the rarified air of estimated prophets, head and shoulders above the rest, the legacy of which had withstood the rigors of race memory. Consequently it was the perfect life, he preached, that should serve as an example for others, rather than a horrific death and spectacular resurrection, even if it was one which would be remembered for thousands of years.

When Yeshua made the divisive statement that he had come to Earth not to bring peace but a sword, it suggested he understood the controversial nature of his ministry. His objective was to reinterpret the Law of Moses, revitalize it, and extend it beyond the tribal bounds to which it was originally set. The sword was a figurative representation of inner conflict. He did not mistake it to be an implement of justice like his contemporaries did. Whereas the scope of the Law of Moses was intended to promote familial and tribal brotherhood, Yeshua sought to extend it beyond these boundaries to promote peace and tranquility on a global scale, bringing together enemies and friends, a new covenant. While his way of provoking change was a peaceful one, he utilized the imagery of the sword to get the point across to his disciples that his ministry was intended to bring about fundamental changes in human behavior that would be met with opposition. He was wise enough to know that when he spoke the following words those who understood them would realize what he meant. The statement followed in Canonical gospel and Gnostic gospel formats.

> *Do not think that I came to bring peace on the earth; I did not come to bring peace, but a sword. For I came to set a man against his father, and a daughter against her mother, and a daughter against her mother-in-law, and a man's enemies will be the members of his household. He who loves father or mother more than me is not worthy of me; and he who loves son or daughter more than me is not worthy of me. And he who does not take his cross and follow after me is not. worthy of me. He who has found his life will lose it, and he who has lost his life for my sake will find it. (Matthew 10:34-39)*

> *Perhaps people think I have come to cast peace upon the world. They do not know that I have come to cast conflicts upon the earth: fire, sword, war. For there will be five in a house: there'll be three against two and two against three, father against son and son against father, and they will stand alone.*
> *(The Gospel of Thomas, non-canonical, Nag Hammadi Anthology)*

Yeshua's way engendered a revolution in social interaction. The idea of offering the other cheek when struck by one's enemy, and forgiving those who trespassed against one, was unthinkable in his day. Retaliation was the order of the day, an eye for an eye and tooth for a tooth. Yeshua realized his effort would not be well-received by the powers-that-be. At their hands, he anticipated his own end because he dared to challenge their interpretation of the Law of Moses. Furthermore he needed to inform his disciples should they be taken by surprise when they met the same fate as he if they preached his message.

Because his message threatened the ideological status quo of the day which was the pecking order of family, tribe, ethnicity, and national identity, it was a danger to it. His teachings inferred a radical change of human perspetive of the prevailing law was imminent, and required to usher in the new era of peace and harmony. However it was a necessary step in human evolution. When the sword of conquest was ultimately replaced by the olive branch of brotherhood, men and women would offer it to each other. That olive branch would be extended to all those who were not members of the same family or tribe or a shared ethnicity. This did not happen in his time, but he offered hope it would happen eventually when the true import of his teachings were understood.

There was a reason why the Jews were still waiting for their messiah to come. No human being could quite measure up to those doctrinal expectations of righteousness, compassion, and Justice anyway. One might assume that was the reason the messiah had not come, but the issue was more complex than that. In their case, a messiah would vanquish their enemies, delivering the faithful from evil. This had not happened yet, and it was doubtful it ever will. Their situation on Earth deteriorated because their obstinacy made more enemies than friends. The Jewish people did not recognize that the Teacher of Righteousness of the Essene had come. Furthermore the Jewish leadership pushed back hard against that idea. They pushed back so hard they ruled that the Romans should crucify him for his supposed blasphemy. That was why the Jews were still waiting. Conceivably they could wait forever. What they asked for they could conceivably do for themselves. But their methodologies seemed to breed more hostilities rather than less. Violence simply begot more violence with no end in sight.

For the Christians, their messiah had come. His First Coming was a dubious success. He spoke the truth, and the enemies of the Light tortured and killed him. Even though his followers pretended his death was by design, it only served to ease a guilty conscience. A rational conclusion was that it was the inevitable cover-up for mishandling his untimely demise. The faithful awaited his return in the form of a Second Coming. However his followers had failed to do what Yeshua expressly told them to do in order to be saved. That was to *"love one another"*. But was a predicted Second Coming that envisioned a triumphant return merely latent disenchantment in one's own performance? Until his commandment was fulfilled, victory could not happen because the pre-requisite had not been met. Then again what they waited for they could conceivably do for themselves. They chose not to for it was a difficult thing to make peace with one's enemy. It was much easier to look to the skies for the coming of the heavenly host to do battle with one's demons, than it was to forgive the transgressions of the ones who were possessed by their own demons. What exactly did one expect a messiah would do for them that they could not do for themselves?

Neither Jews nor Christians could probably handle the shock when the epiphany dawned that the messiah was already here and he lay dormant in each one of us. He was not a person but a spiritual force of Nature, namely the Christ Consciousness. This force had always been with us. It had never left here so it could not return here. It was the Light of the human spirit. The faithful wait for the messiah to reveal himself, so it was very unlikely he or she would actually recognize him when he did. He hid in plain sight as the faithful looked past him, and concocted their own glorious vision of the Christ as the conquistador. Sadly that was a desire for Justice that will never be fulfilled in the manner they desired. They waited for a Second Coming of the Messiah which had already occurred. His resurrection from the dead was that Second Coming. A third coming was never predicted. Therefore there was no point in waiting for it to happen. In the entirety of the provisions for deliverance made in the Book of REVELATION, there was no provision made for a Third Coming of the Christ.

The Christ had no part in turning his mission into a resurrection cult. That was not his intent. His intent was to create a model for the living faith like any good rabbi would. The Christ's supposed progeny in Rome tried to incorporate his message into a resurrection cult because the message evolved. It evolved naturally like an Evangelical mission would. The Christian faith was catapulted into the stratosphere on the wings of resurrection, martyrdom, and life everlasting. It was the engine that supplied the fuel of faith that was required to reach the promised land of the after-life. As time went on, the after-life in heaven became more of a goal than living itself, and preparing for it became the actual purpose of life itself. A striving for perfection usurped the throne of humankind's desires to understand life, its process and purpose. In the interim, the faithful forgot how the Christ taught them to live. It was easier to adhere to the resurrection model, and await his return. It was a return that would never come. Hence, theists sit at the crossroads of the Ages pondering which road to take, not fully aware that all roads lead to the same place.

At issue was whether institutionalizing the Church doctrine damaged the Christ's message and goals. How far from its original message had the Church strayed? Was it true to the teachings of the Christ? What kind of mind did the Church create? What kind of mind should Yeshua's teachings create? The remainder of this book will delve into an examination of the prevailing spiritual mentality.

Chapter 23 THE CHILDREN OF THE LAW OF ONE

THE CHILDREN OF THE LAW OF ONE were alleged to be a group of survivors who fled the continent of Atlantis during the final phases of its destruction approximately 11,500 years ago. They settled initially in Egypt among other places on the African, North American, South American, and European continents. To Egypt under the leadership of Thoth, they brought with them the spiritual teachings of the elders of Atlantis. These teachings were revealed in the ancient mysteries of Universal Law and the Seven Laws of Creation (Order, Balance, Harmony, Growth, God-Perception, Love, and Compassion). In short, they taught that God, they termed the ALL-IN-ALL, was One, and that every physical manifestation of the Universe emanated from One Source. It was manifested in accordance with the principle of *as above, so below* and was dispersed throughout the Universe. Their expressed purpose was to teach the Truth and thereby fulfill their mandate to show the way back to union with the One.

The Atlantean survivors were later to be labeled the Watchers in the Hebrew BOOK OF ENOCH, and the Sumerian epic of GILGAMESH by those who they watched. The human beings were a race of adolescents by comparison: they being the ones that were being watched. Why they were being watched was not known to them, only that they were. The motives of the watchers were suspect because as these sources so crudely put it -- the watchers were also associated with the so-called *giants who lusted after the daughters of men*. The word *giant* was an obvious mistranslation. A more appropriate word to use, inferring their stature, was *titans* as the Greeks used in their mythology. It noted their intellectual superiority, rather than their physical size. However as any explorers would be, the watchers had been sent on a mission to scope out the territory, investigate the indigenous tribes, and make a determination if colonization was a viable possibility. Lascivious intent was not their primary motivation. It was only what it resulted in from the perspective of those who were being watched. Due to their limited intelligence, the human beings could not conceive of any other motivation that did not relate directly to them. Except for the education of Enoch by an angel named Uriel, no other motivation was known, or even hinted at by their association. So it was a matter of perspective that came across in the historical record. Reportedly the details of the Atlantean civilization were contained in the Library of Alexandria. Those records were lost when the Romans burned it to the ground during their conquest of Egypt in the 2nd Century of the Common Era.

Thoth was an Atlantean who survived the destruction of Atlantis by escaping to a colony founded in Egypt. It might also be inferred it was unlikely he traveled there alone. The ancient wisdom of THE CHILDREN OF THE LAW OF ONE traveled to Egypt with him, as well as an entourage from the Temple of the Living Spirit. There was little to add except to say that if Atlantis was as advanced a civilization as it was said to be, anything was possible. Advanced civilizations tended to expand their domain at will. In contemporary times, it was called manifest destiny. Colonization and commerce tended to go hand-in-hand. Atlantean technology was said to employ lasers, crystals, magnetism, and electricity. If they could harness the atom, store data in crystals, or travel on electrical impulses through a magnetic field, they could certainly build ships that could travel great distances on the water or through the air. Perhaps they could even travel into outer space. If so, no one should doubt they had access to the entire planet by air or sea, and having this capability it was perfectly reasonable they would use it. No more compelling reason could there be but to flee to safety while their continent was being destroyed by natural disasters.

As psychically-conversant as they were, they no

doubt had a premonition of the imminent series of calamities that would befall their continent. As scientifically advanced as they were, it was likely they used their technology to ensure safe passage for as many as possible. There was no esoteric meaning to be found here, just sound reasoning. It was logical to assume the Atlanteans believed that to save the best of their civilization, the best they could do was to transplant it somewhere else. Their pinnacle of accomplishment in philosophy was the teachings of THE CHILDREN OF THE LAW OF ONE. Preserving them would be high on their list of priorities at least for the priests in the Temple of the Living Spirit. If it was appropriate to save anything from Atlantis one would assume that, was it.

The concept of *as above, so below* was older than any civilization humanity possessed any records of. It predated known history, and because it did few lent any credence to this concept as being viable. *As above, so below* was the universal rule proposed by a man known as Hermes Trismegistus and was ultimately the product of the Hermetic school of philosophy that bore his name. He was considered to be the first Egyptian. That was to say his advent on the scene was the spark that ignited a cultural bang in Egypt. In Egyptian mythology, he was given credit for the rise of the Egyptian civilization. In terms of mythology it was believed there was always a thread of truth to it however slight. In a single generation, a nation of hunters and gatherers were poised to ascend to the top rung of Mediterranean civilizations. A village of mud huts was transformed into a metropolis of magnificent temples within a century. Egypt's meteoric rise to prominence was due to a transplant of Atlantean culture and philosophy.

The indigent population (those who occupied the land when he arrived there) depicted him as coming from a land beyond the setting sun. One day he appeared among them. They named him a god, Thoth or Tehuti, a lord of wisdom and learning. It was because his genius surpassed theirs, not because he was an actual god. Because in every way his skills surpassed theirs, it was evident he knew much more than they would ever know.

In Egyptian mythology, Thoth governed over mystical wisdom, magic, writing, and other artistic disciplines and was associated with healing, while Hermes was credited with being the personification of universal wisdom and messenger of the gods in Greek mythology. He was also the patron of magic. It was only those who did not have clear understanding of the mandate of Universal Law that believed in magic. There was nothing in it that either defied logic or appeared inscrutable to one who had his or her finger upon the pulse of the heartbeat of universal force and intelligence. The level of mastery attained was due to achievement through learning and growing rather than endowment as if receiving a gift of grace from unseen forces. It was a perspective that had been intentionally lost over the millennia. His wisdom was hidden from the masses by those who wished to keep knowledge under lock and key. In Egypt, a priest class arose to jealously guard the secret wisdom lest it became common knowledge.

Some psychics maintained the entire catalog of Hermes' writings, notwithstanding the HERMETICA, was lost when the Library of Alexandria was burned to the ground in the second century of the Common Era. The Roman emperor Diocletian razed it during his conquest of Egypt. Quite probably he did not know or care it was a library or what it contained. Being a Roman he probably felt all the knowledge and culture the world needed Rome already had. His rationale perhaps was not fully realizing much of the culture Rome did have was appropriated from Greek civilization which had appropriated much of it from Egyptian civilization. By a sort of cultural osmosis, civilization was often passed on. With the loss of the Library at Alexandria, the loss to humankind was incalculable. If it had been known who Hermes/Thoth was, where he came from, and what he knew, the mystery of human pre-history would have been exposed. The ravages of Time had claimed great civilizations so it was not unreasonable to believe that would include great ideas as well. Humanity could not even imagine what was lost because in order to know that would require knowledge it did not ever possess. The teachings of Hermes or what was known of them mirrored the teachings of THE CHILDREN OF THE LAW OF ONE. That stands to reason since he was affiliated with that group.

With the destruction of the Library at Alexandria, Hermes Trismegistus (Hermes thrice-greatest) became one of those historical personages lost in the fog of Time. His contribution to humanity was now considered to be a product of mythology. Reportedly for one who was considered by many to be a fictional character, Hermes was a prolific writer. His accomplishments were legendary almost to the point few would believe one man could accomplish them. Hermes was credited with writing 20,000 books by Iamblichus, circa 250-300 BCE, a neo-platonic Syrian philosopher, and over 36,000 books by Manetho, circa 300

BCE, an Egyptian priest who wrote the history of Egypt in Greek, perhaps for Ptolemy I. In the combined mythology of two individuals, Thoth and Hermes, who purportedly were the same person, it was reported that both Thoth and Hermes revealed to humanity the healing arts, magic, writing, astrology, science, and philosophy.

According to legend, Hermes Trismegistus was said to have provided the wisdom of light in the ancient mysteries of Egypt. Reportedly he carried an emerald upon which was recorded the substance of his philosophical beliefs, and the caduceus, the symbol of mystical illumination. He vanquished Typhon, the dragon of ignorance, and mental, moral, and physical perversion. Physical perversion was a latent reference to Egyptian mythology which featured creatures that were half-man and half-beast. The Nubus and the Sphinx were prime examples of what had come down to humanity in the form of mythology. Whether it was mythology or actual physical perversion was unverifiable at this time. But mythological references to creatures of this kind were prevalent throughout the annals of early Mediteranean civilizations – primarily the Babylonians, Egyptians, Greeks, Romans, and Sumerians. Was it a case of actual experience in pre-historical times or evidence of civilizations copying each other's experience and recording it as their own? Hermes' only known surviving work was the HERMETICA, a collection of 42 books that had profoundly influenced the development of Western occultism and magic. Reputedly the Egyptian Tarot was one of his many inventions that survived today.

    Purportedly the Law of One constituted the main body of teachings of the elders of the Atlantean race. Hence it was reasonable to assume it was appropriate to draw a correlation between them because much of the terminology used was the same. To believe they were one and same without comparing texts might be a stretch of the imagination when it was primarily based on inference. However, much of the Earth's biological history was pieced together by a fossil record, and gaps in the linear historical timelines were filled in by implication. Therefore who was to say what was contrived and what was not. Often what separated mythology from historical fact was the intellectual honesty of the contemporary historian. Some ancients had it, others did not because they were not privy to esoteric teachings. Incorporating enough of the human element in one's mythology made it appealing to humanity, but did not make it qualify as Truth.

It was said Hermes carried an emerald upon which was inscribed the essence of his philosophy with the caduceus, the symbol of mystical illumination. The reason the emerald tablet was known today was because knowledge of it survived as part of the **HERMETICA**. The stone was inscribed in Phoenician, and purportedly revealed the secrets of the universe. The inscription was later translated in the Arabic languages and Greek. The inscription on the emerald tablet read: *"That which is above is like that which is below and that which is below is like that which is above, to achieve the wonders of the One Thing. This is the foundation of astrology and alchemy: that the microcosm of mankind and the earth is a reflection of the macrocosm of God and the heavens"*. Reportedly the entire system of traditional and modern magic was inscribed upon the emerald tablet in cryptic wording. Whether it was the obscurity of the translation or the difficulty of deciphering it, there was little on it that appeared to make sense to contemporary thinkers. Classical esotericism theorized its true meaning that must be found in every human's soul. Hence the meaning was elicited from the soul's remembrance, rather than the mind's thought process. The message of the emerald tablet read as follows: *"True,* *without falsehood, certain and most true, that which is above is the same as that which is below, and that which is below is the same as that which is above, for the performance of miracles of the One Thing. And as all things have their birth from this One Thing by adaptation, the Sun is its Father, the Moon its Mother, the Wind carries it in its belly, and its nurse is the Earth. This is the Father of all perfection, or consummation of the whole world. Its power is integrating, if it be turned into earth. You shall separate the earth from the fire, the subtle from the gross, suavely, and with great ingenuity and skill. Your skillful work ascends from earth to heaven and descends to the earth again, and receives the power of the superiors and of the inferiors. So thou hast the glory of the whole world – therefore let all obscurity flee from thee. This is the strong force of all forces, overcoming every subtle and penetrating every solid thing. So the world was created. Hence all were wonderful adaptations, of which this is the manner. Therefore I am Hermes Trismegistus having the three parts of the philosophy of the whole world. What I have to tell is completed concerning the Operation of the Sun."*

The Emerald Tablet was said to have been discovered in a caved tomb, clutched in the hands of the corpse of Hermes. Legends differed on the discoverer. One said it was Sarah, the wife of Abraham. Another attributed it to Apollonius of Tyana. The nature of legends being as they may, no one knew for a certainty which was true, or if there was another possible explanation. According to annals of THE CHILDREN OF THE LAW OF ONE, neither explanation could be true because Hermes left Egypt prior to his death and settled in Tibet. Furthermore whether an entire system of magic could be inscribed on the emerald was another topic for debate. It was mentioned in this text because of the philosophical link between Apollonius and Yeshua, and that was enough to suggest its relevance to the teachings of the Essene and its Teacher of Righteousness.

The conceptual meaning of the phrase, *as above, so below*, was summarized in the inscription on the emerald tablet that Hermes carried. It was believed to hold the key to all mysteries. It was said all systems of magic function on the basis of this formula: *"That which is above is the same as that which is below. Macrocosms is the same as microcosmos. The universe is the same as God. God is the same as man. Man is the same as the cell; the cell is the same as the atom, and so forth ad infinitum."*

The preceding statement theorized that man was the

counterpart of God on Earth, as God was man's counterpart in heaven. Therefore it was a statement of an ancient belief (of Atlantean origin, it was proposed) that man's actions on Earth paralleled the actions of God in heaven. This belief pivoted upon the proposition that *"all things have their birth from this One Thing by adaptation"*. Mind and body, galaxy and atom, sensation and stimulus were intimately bound. The mystic quality in spiritualism strongly imbued the view that all things at once, were independent and interrelated, differentiated as well as integrated. These concepts pivoted upon the belief that all things came from the One Thing, or First Cause, and its power was integrating, if it be focused on spirit or matter.

The purpose of all rituals in ceremonial mysticism was to unite the microcosm with the macrocosm, to join the human consciousness with the Universal consciousness. When such a union was achieved the subject and object became one. This was because the mystic felt he or she was consciously in touch with all elements of the universe. This feeling intensified the more the mystic successfully practiced his or her craft. Whenever failures occurred, one knew the ritual was not performed correctly. When feeling in unison with the universe the mystic knew he or she had reached his or her higher or true self because one had attained mastery of the connection between oneself and the universe. Thus one felt one's skillful work *"ascends from Earth to heaven and descends to Earth again, and receives the power of the superiors and of the inferiors"* as Hermes said. Therefore, one *"hast the glories of the whole world therefore let all obscurity flee from thee."* Now the miracles were possible.

As light required darkness to complete the day, so the Children had their enemy. It was a small group of their number who had adopted a perversion of the Law of One. In their case, the *one* was the self. To use a Star Wars analogy, they were the dark side of the Force, the children of Belial. In the communal literature of the Essene, the children of Belial were mentioned as well. They were just as powerful and just as dedicated to their cause. Furthermore they had deceived a multitude of human beings to follow them. What they had to offer was the same thing that the devil tempted Yeshua with during his 40 days in the wilderness: pleasure, power, riches, and world domination. With their deceit and guile they were a formidable adversary, and then as now by all accounts they had won over a large percentage of the human population to their cause. They offered what the vainglorious craved: ego-lust and narcissism. Love of self and mammon with an appetite for destruction was the sum total of their credo. It appealed to those who desired carte blanche to feed their egos to the bursting point without any checks and balances to subdue the urge.

Underlying this also was the recognition of an eternal battle between the Children of the Law of One and the Children of Belial. It would be appropriate to view this as an analogy of the traditional conflict between Light and Darkness, or spiritualism and materialism. The writings of the Essene sect were filled with references to the sons of light and the sons of darkness, and the inevitable battle between them. They are now known as the Dead Sea scrolls, but they were the Bible of their day. All fables or myths had an element of truth in them, not because of who told them, but because of where they came from – a subconscious remembrance of days gone by. They often instilled a foreboding of days to come. Latent in the collective unconscious as a race memory was this battle which was carried down to humanity as a fable like that of the conflict between God and Satan. From that conflict the fallen angels or agents of Belial worked in earnest to separate humanity from Spiritual Law, while the children or agents of the One worked in earnest to rejoin humanity to Spiritual Law. Each side endeavored to swell its ranks, the objective being to control the destiny of the human race.

Truly it was the battle of the ages, at the center of which was control of the human thought process, and subsequently the fate of the human individual. Ultimately this dovetailed into the fate of the human race as a whole, and Nature itself. One could imagine angels and demons casting lots for human souls, exchanging universal consciousness for separate consciousness respectively. But a game of chance it was not because as one heart was reclaimed at a time from the refuse pile, the balance shifted in the positive direction. Conversely the opposite was true. As the influence on the human mind meandered between these poles of influence, the magnetic pull of each registered in the human soul. While choice was the determining factor, the field of choices was pre-determined. They encompassed the full range of Creation, but light and darkness could not cohabitate the same space at the same time. In effect, the expression of each cancelled the other out if they cohabitated, rendering the space null and void.

In the book of REVELATION, the writer substituted another name for Belial, the force of ego, dubbing it The

Beast. It came to power when it joined forces with The Harlot (the facilitator of ideology). That could be interpreted to be the backing The Beast got from the human expression of government, press, clergy, and economic interests because they each wanted a piece of what the strategies of manifest destiny offered. That was – you could keep what you claimed for your own. But it seemed the real meaning the book of REVELATION was lost on them because they were all distracted by the heavy-handed good versus evil scenario. That was not the issue at all. Good and evil were only value judgments. The issue was living one's life in accordance with the spirit of giving, versus living one's life in accordance with the spirit of taking. For this reason THE CHILDREN OF THE LAW OF ONE had created the Path back to the Light of spiritual essence. Thus they taught principle and how to bring oneself into alignment with it. The Children of Belial wanted to keep humanity anchored in the darkness of matter. Thus they taught substance and how to manipulate it. Both meanings had been taken out of context and immersed in competing ideologies so that one must choose between them to be saved or damned. All that was really meant by it was a choice of returning to the One or remaining in separateness.

Consequently a magical, mystical meaning was

sought that was couched in mystery so that only the initiated could understand it. Originally the book of REVELATION was a coded message for the faithful. It advised them to keep the faith, and know that divine retribution for the pain they suffered was at-hand if they kept to the Path. In essence, the message it provided was that the devil was a worthy adversary, but God would prevail in the end. In the lingo of the Law of One it meant that light would overwhelm darkness. Without light there would be no consciousness of life. Pure principle was the progenitor to its subordinate manifestations. Desire was relative while principle was constant. Attraction and repulsion, electricity, and electromagnetism were physical manifestations of universal force. Universal Law was derived from an understanding of the operation of these forces, both spiritually and materially.

By contrast the message provided by the CHILDREN OF THE LAW OF ONE had deeper significance than that a simple outline of the battle of good versus evil. It clearly defined the aspects of Christ Consciousness and anti-Christ Consciousness and inferred how to recognize each. The difference could be demonstrated in the simple phrase: The anti-Christ was merely the opposite of the Christ. It could be delineated by saying: the Christ operated within the Law, and the anti-Christ operated outside of it. The Christ had no possessions. Conversely the anti-Christ wanted all of them. The Christ strove for unity. Conversely the anti-Christ strove for divisiveness. While the Christ preached the brotherhood of Man, the anti-Christ wanted men to seek dominance over each other. The Christ wanted you to share your abundance with everyone else. Conversely the anti-Christ wanted you to hoard everything for yourself. This was not a hard thing to figure out, at least for one who knew what the Christ Consciousness was really all about.

The task was to look at it as objectively as possible without getting caught up in the subjectivity of expressing likes and dislikes as human beings were wont to do. A preference for one ideology over the other was a pointless exercise in one-upmanship. Its purpose was to keep humanity arguing the fine points of faith amongst themselves so that they will never unite in a common purpose to observe the Law of One. Therefore the concept of ideologies competing for the favor of the Father meant not a single one of them would lead to the One. They would all lead away from it as was the plan of the Children of Belial.

Chapter 24 Applying The Law Of One

The operating principles of THE CHILDREN OF THE LAW OF ONE were the same as those of the Great White Brotherhood and the Essene. They were the tenets of Universal Law. It was that set of parameters translated into material and spiritual functions by which the Universe and every bit of creative energy within it operated. Among them were the laws governing cause and effect, attraction and repulsion, and the management of electrical impulse by which every bit of matter and spirit in the universe were governed. Traditionally there were seven laws or principles of Universal Law. The Universe existed in perfect harmony by virtue of these Laws. Ancient mystical, esoteric and secret teachings dating back over 5,000 years from Ancient Egypt to Ancient Greece and to the Vedic tradition of Ancient India corroborated their existence. They were described as follows and they interoperated to produce consciousness and the movement of consciousness through the stages of personal development. Each law built upon the other.

The first law was the law of mentalism. It denoted that thought was life. Consciousness was the progenitor of manifestation. The path from collective unconscious to subconscious to ego-consciousness was a continuous stream of motion. Wisdom was downloaded from the collective unconscious to the human mind. While the human mind had the ability to think, the human essence intimated that it was primed with thought-forms from the Divine. Their assumption was that minds properly focused helped men and women to lead more virtuous lives. Homegrown reasoning capability was enhanced when it was founded upon virtuous conduct.

The second law was the law of correspondence. It literally meant, *as above, so below*, that which was reflected in the Ideal or spiritual realm was brought into existence in the Real or physical realm. What was imaged into the mind was the source of manifestation. Greek and Egyptian Hermeticism were ingrained with a similar concept. The flow of energy was transmuted via the DNA constructs throughout Creation, downloaded from the Cosmos into every living thing. The process of spiritual alchemy imbued the cells of living things with spiritual force. That spiritual force was transformed into physical reality by intelligence resident in each cell. Thus from One came many permutations as aptly expressed in the aphorism, *Out of many, One*, in other words, E Pluribus Unum.

The third law was the law of vibration. It denoted that

feeling drove thought. It meant pure energy vibrated eternally. Energy was in a perpetual state of transmigration. It was not created or destroyed. It manifested in forms. Vibration manifested in different forms due to the Universe being a vast, efficient recycling engine. Vedic traditions endorsed the same conceptual view of vibration. Vibration was a continuous wave. It was the building block. It was the source of life and reason for life, all at the same time. The tone and frequency of vibration provided a diversity of life forms. Each permutation of vibrational difference exhibited a singularity of nuance and substance.

The fourth law was the law of polarity. It meant energy congealed or it dispersed. The magnetic force generated caused negative and positive energies to attract and repel. By magnetic polarization, energy was congealed into matter, or it could cause it to fly apart. Bits and pieces of the One, or singularity, were held together or separated by magnetic force whether applied consciously or unconsciously.

The fifth law was the law of rhythm. It meant the pulse of the beat of life caused energy to move consciousness. As all things flowed in and out, up and down, and across, matter and energy was provided movement. The prime mover, as

Aristotle called it, caused a continuous stream of motion on the grid of the Universe. It was an eternal ebb and flow. Metaphorically that prime mover was considered to be the hand of God.

The sixth law was the law of cause and effect. It meant every action had a reaction. As consciousness made choices, matter responded. Every singularity responded to the ebb and flow of conscious or unconscious symmetrical motion. Virtuous conduct then was a result of cosmic symmetry. Immoral conduct was a result of cosmic asymmetry. Balance and harmony were maintained by the equilibrium of giving and taking. The practices of spiritual alchemy were utilized to synchronize human life with spiritual life and promote balance and harmony.

The seventh law was the law of gender. It meant masculine and feminine principles exist in everything to provide a balance of give and take, repulsion and absorption, hostility and receptivity, and aggression and submission. The yin and yang of cosmic lore was given expression in every action and reaction. The perfect assimilation of masculine and feminine attributes lent itself to a more perfect expression of love.

One thing was for certain. It was no mean feat to walk

the straight-and-narrow path of THE CHILDREN OF THE LAW OF ONE. While it was easy for a human being to yield to the material desires of pleasure and pain, it was hard to transcend them. The path of spiritual endeavor was a long arduous one, the reward for which was not immediately evident or tangible. Selflessness often was not. The path offered by selfishness was a short-cut often showing immediate results. But it was a transitory gain. It ebbed and flowed with the tide of cause and effect given expression by the circumstances offered in lifetimes human beings must all endure. They chose their path from the smorgasbord laid out, and paid for it thereafter with every breath they took. It was much later in the process of life that one may experience buyer's remorse. But by then it was too late to undo the damage that one had wrought, but it was never too late to alter one's course.

  Until one stopped listening to the ego that was in a panic because whatever it got was never enough, one was ensnared in its grasp. The way was blocked by its desires. When one started listening to the higher mind which told you that the love in your heart was enough, the way was cleared. As Thoth suggested, *now the miracles begin*. And the first miracle came when one had the epiphany that each individual *was one and the same* even if they were physically separate. Each succeeding *miracle* depended upon how one applied that knowledge in the form of behavioral modifications. The true miracle of life was achieved when one comprehended the dichotomy of sameness and individuality, and manifested an appropriate change in behavior. That change in behavior revealed one got it.

The Law of One was the root of human scientific endeavor as well as its belief systems. It was not intended to replace the wisdom or guidance that could be offered by a true teacher. It was being offered in lieu of one. Among other things their instructions indicated was that one must will to be one's own messiah. The salvation offered by religious ideology may provide temporary emotional relief, but in reality, it was merely an attempt at mind-control perpetuated by those who had something to gain. Be it material abundance or the warm feeling inside you got when you perceived you were helping someone else see the light. Its value was in stimulating the spirit within to move. In the long run, no one was being helped for long if they were taken by the hand. This type of selfless service was an indulgence for failure to comprehend the Universal Mind offered by those who were not necessarily empowered to provide it. Its effectiveness was directly proportional to one's propensity for self-delusion. It was never going to supplant the need for purposeful action on the seeker's part. That action you had to supply of your own volition. If you did not speak for yourself, who would speak for you? If you did not act for yourself, who would act on your behalf? Life was a continuous stream of action and reaction within a river that flowed. Therefore one was not ever absolved of the responsibility for the choices they had made. One was simply required to make a choice. Then as Thoth suggested, the miracles began.

No matter what the derivation was of the OneThing, the understanding of its composition could not be accomplished without significant effort. That effort was being trained upon the intersecting lines of force among God, Man and Nature. It was central to possessing a core of Idealism upon which to draw. For one to be able to produce that which was real, one had to understand the Ideal from which it came. This was where the teachings of THE CHILDREN OF THE LAW OF ONE came into play, and showed Yeshua was preaching their faith to humanity. They were older than mankind itself, being delivered from the Other Side, and being taught in an oral tradition since the dawn of Time by the Great White Brotherhood. They had been carried through the Ages and delivered to humanity by every major religion and by every major prophet or Adept who received it directly from the Source. These teachings were the undercurrent of philosophy of force and intelligence of the ONE itself which manifested in the expression of the one commandment – Love. The prophet of every Age had always carried the message of the One.

For our current age, this prophet, Yeshua the Christ, carried the message of *love one another.* No other precept of moral code preempted it. No other precept of ethics was required to enable it. It stood alone as the enabling rule of Natural Law. Universal Law worked in concert to manifest it. These included all laws of attraction and repulsion, cause and effect, and spiritual or material force and intelligence. They all melded into the One, being its expression. And if humanity was to follow this commandment with its full force of spirit in the spirit it was given, salvation as offered by religion was unnecessary. It was this sustaining and life-giving message to all humanity that provided so-called salvation. It was the only edict to follow.

All of the perversions of faith, doctrine, and misguided ideology would inevitably fall away and the clear light of transcendental wisdom would prevail. But that would not happen without the human input to the equation. Therefore one must put one's shoulder to the Wheel to move the mountain or it will not move. It could not without the force behind it. Life was never intended to be a spectator sport. One must act. What was given was really earned. It was a function of cause and effect. One's body of work, their so-called karma, was the baggage one carried from womb to tomb. It was only the misgivings of the separate-but-equal philosophy that declared spiritualism and materialism inhabit distinctly different planes of existence. It was the imbalance between them that kept humanity in bondage. The belief that the twain-shall-never-meet ensured one would never be free from a life of toil and travail. There was always work to do, but if one had love in one's heart it was not a chore, but a blessing.

Chapter 25 Opening A Vista On The True Faith

A heavenly reward did not await the faithful, any more than a hellish one awaited the unfaithful. It was a scare tactic levied at humanity by the purveyors of religious doctrine. If meeting the expectation of morally-acceptable behavior was the only prerequisite for being welcomed by St. Peter at the heavenly gates, then humanity as a race should be considered no better schooled than domesticated animals performing for treats. A preoccupation with the concepts of heaven and hell, or everlasting joy versus everlasting torment, did not instill in the individual the proper focus; for they were empty threats aimed at leveraging the quality of conviction, nothing more, nothing less.

In meeting temptation head-on to defeat it, the theist was ill-equipped with a pocketbook full of aphorisms, and an understanding of shallow waters. The spoon-feeding of the theist served only to create a false sense of security that was quickly dispelled in times of crisis. While one may be able to regurgitate doctrine when prompted, that did not ensure one understood what one was required to ingest. There were a great many of the faithful who were adept at reciting biblical passages at the ready, but the true test of their understanding was the quality of the life they led.

The true test was whether or not one practiced what one preached, and its measurement was the quality of character one exhibited. When the bar was set too high for anyone to climb over it, most were satisfied to crawl underneath it. If they strayed, they repented their sin, and this served to keep them in the fold.

As a result, all religious systems had eventually sunk into ego-worship of Master entities to get closer to the Truth through the one who lived it. The theist could not even imagine a life without their guidance. When a man was taught to adhere to doctrine instead of trusting his own intuition, he was not positioned to trust his own opinion. Thus it did position him to trust his neighbor's opinion either, especially if that neighbor did not share his faith. Inevitably the theist would misunderstand the message because one did not listen with one's heart. Then the arguments would ensue over the interpretation of the words one heard. Thus instead of desiring to optimize oneself, the theist wished to become someone else, longing to be born-again with a new identity. Thus out of necessity, the born-again mentality was born.

In modern times, the fundamentalists of all persuasions look through the simple truth without perceiving it, and complicate the lives of all concerned with literal translations of words and phrases borrowed from the echoes of a distant past. From the ranks of false prophets were many who aspired to the rank of an Anointed One, but were defeated by their own materialism. Even the most eloquent lies of priests, ministers, rabbis, and imams could be stripped naked by the discriminating mind. A genuine man of God was well aware that the pulpit was not the place for rallying to the cause of personal or political agendas. But that did not stop the unscrupulous from seizing the opportunity to corrupt the unwitting and energize them in the pursuit of a Golden Calf. Such vested interests were prime real estate in the land that Time forgot.

    The so-called truth religious authorities of all persuasions had stamped with a seal of approval was little more than settling for a lesser goal of sanitized faith. The effort expended to perpetuate the half-truth served to convince the foolish that it should be believed. Unfortunately, there were some who would believe the explanations of any vestige of authority no matter how absurd or harmful its claims may be. The greater the lie it seemed, the more fools knelt before it. This was indicative of the epidemic of desperate measures with which many seemed to be afflicted.

With the emptiness they felt in their hearts yearning to be filled, they would drink the coarse desert sand if it was made appealing enough. In the lieu of Truth, the half-truth becomes a plausible alternative, and the more it was complicated, the more plausible it became to the ignorant among men.

There will always be questions to be asked in the shadow of the half-truth, and when they cannot be answered by the inquirer himself or herself, one will inevitably seek them from perceived authorities. Though these answers appeared to be heartfelt responses at the time they were offered, they often proved to be empty promises of salvation from those not qualified to give them. Often, they proved to be nothing more than sanctioned, canned responses to those who petitioned Authority for meaning.

Even Evangelism had its limits of personal commitment and endurance, and there came a time when it no longer satisfied. The novelty wore off, and one was left with nests full of fledglings clamoring for *mama* to feed them their daily bread. Emotional extravaganzas were not meant to convey any message attributed to the Word of God. They were entertainment for the masses, a stimulus to hold one's interest while salvation was being marketed, unfortunately many times for the least spiritual of reasons.

Both the Gnostics and the Essene contended no one had an inherent right to bias an expression of faith with scripted messages and contrived doctrine. To them, the profiteers of faith discredited the solemn Word of God by playing to the audience, giving them a good show rather than what they needed. Joy was not a prerequisite for faith especially when it was elicited on cue by the performance of evangelist entertainers. Gratitude for a fine performance filled the collection plate, but it did not effectively make the case for salvation. No rational individual would be so moved to embrace a performance and use it as a foundation upon which to base their faith. It was only the desperate believers who applauded such efforts, while the rational adherents needed to be convinced no further, and were rarely moved an inch.

Periodically one may need a renewal of one's commitment; for one was but a human being who required reassurance his or her efforts were on the right track. Understandably the typical human being felt far less confidant and comfortable in the company of strangers than friends. Thus a congregation consensus served a useful purpose in reinforcing one's belief. Comradeship in spirit provided a valuable opportunity for the faithful to bolster one another's articles of faith, and the intent was not to demean its significance. The concern arose only when the accent was upon conformity rather than ingenuity. When it was preferable to blend in with the crowd rather than stand out, it was wise for one to let one's conscience be one's guide.

The abuses of overbearing sects like the Moonies, the People's Temple, Heaven's Gate, or the Branch Davidians had become so severe that it was wise to be ever vigilant one was not a pawn in another's shell game. The perpetuation of moral crimes in the name of God under the auspices of tribal faith should never be mistaken for the true path. Unfortunately history was full of examples that would lead one to believe it was the modus operandi for all time. Unconscionable zealotry had often been the excuse for such abuses of power as if it was an acceptable alibi for them. But sanctioned persecutions and inquisitions of so-called heretics did not serve to purify the tribal faith as may be suggested to justify them. And they were especially heinous when motivated by a bizarre sense of justice like in the case of the Spanish Inquisition. They simply tarnished the altruistic aims of the truly righteous proponents of religious faith for all time.

Furthermore they served as a reminder that many

were not as steadfast or confident in their articles of faith as they would like to pretend. If one felt the urgency to homogenize the tribe, a red flag should be raised. Most importantly it emboldened the fascist elements of every religious persuasion who had ingratiated themselves into the mainstream of religious practice, to spread their message of hate and fear. They perverted the expression of faith with their distorted views of doctrine and extremist behavior that incited paranoia within the rank and file. Further polarization only served the needs of the radical element to seize control of a righteous cause that set the tribe on a perilous course to denigrate its altruistic aim. The radicalization of legitimate faith was the proof that sectarianism was truly the mother of strife. The wise knew all too well if zealotry was permitted to fester within the ranks, it would eventually lead to the obliteration of the true faith.

    Seemingly the theist had been deluded into believing that God only represented a force of good and that a force of evil, called the devil, the adversary, worked in opposition to HIM. If God was ONE, this could not be true. It would mean God was divided against HIMSELF and that IT consciously permitted this to happen. What they did not seem to recognize was that God was the All-in-All as the Great White

Brotherhood and Essene asserted, and consequently could not be subdivided into ideological components. God represented the total package, or IT represented nothing at all. However instead of recognizing this simple statement of fact, ecumenical hypotheses were concocted to explain the mysterious confluence of good and evil forces. It revealed a glaring inconsistency in the doctrine of Orthodox faiths which they seemingly failed to realize. The so-called evil they witnessed existed in a portion of humanity that chose to pervert the God-force within them to attain their own selfish ends. Thus egoistic behavior was perceived as evil because it was contrary to the instructions of the spiritual DNA. Hence those who believed in the fallacy of the devil fail to observe the Law of One, preferring to fracture it into cleverly-crafted ecumenical treatises. It left them to piece together the jagged parts of a puzzle, which in all probability they would rearrange in the wrong order. It was readily apparent they did not know God and pretended to neither serve nor understand the universal laws of cause and effect which set them in motion.

In the meantime, the whispers of the secrets of the ages had become little more than a rumor of treasure. Mysticism of all kinds, being founded upon secrets, was jealously guarded. Secret societies arose for the expressed purpose of keeping knowledge hidden from those who would misuse it. Rituals were practiced behind closed doors by the select few. Lest one be worthy one was not permitted on the path. In essence the purpose was to find and express Truth. Not everyone was deemed worthy to find the Holy Grail of the Secrets of the Ages. The problem was who decided who was worthy and who was not. Often it was those who had ulterior motives for making those decisions. Most often the purpose was as much to retain an advantage over one's fellows, as it was to keep the knowledge from those who would pervert it. Civilizations had risen and fallen because too few were privy to the knowledge required to perpetuate them. They rotted from within out of fear of being conquered from without. The faiths of these civilizations were all founded upon a false premise that knowledge should not be freely given to whoever asked for it.

No ruler was needed when any human being was capable of ruling. The only qualification should be that one was a sincere seeker of high moral fiber. But instead the qualifications enforced were piety, obedience, and loyalty. Throughout the ages, these prerequisites were cited as virtues when they were not virtues at all. They were assurances that hierarchical allegiances were observed and the walls of the holy of holies of any faith were not breached by the unworthy. However the truth of the matter was no one was truly unworthy of receiving one's birthright provided one was pure of heart. That should be the only qualification. Even then, that test of character was not always predicated upon an honest appraisal. Human beings driven by emotion more than principle caused likes and dislikes too often to get in the way. Their vision was clouded by prerequisites that preferred filial association and ideological concurrence to merit and character. It was based upon an assumption that one's worth was predicated upon how one measured up in the eyes of others. That assumed the assessment was always unbiased and sincere, but it rarely was.

Being a case in point, the concept of attaining Christ Consciousness was thought to be reserved for the Elect, the anointed ones, but according to universal law it was the path each soul was destined to travel. That message was lost in translation. Furthermore the path was available to all who requested it. As the masters had always said: "*ask and you shall receive*", but one was free to ask for whatever they desired as often as they desired it. No qualifications were ever placed upon the requestors that were not within reach by choice. No knowledge was hidden unless one made the effort to hide it. The key to unlock knowledge was turned by one's understanding, and the effort one made to attain it. Barricades had been erected that required demands from the seeker before he or she was allowed to turn the key. First and foremost was the oath one may be obligated to swear before the Idol of mystery. It was that the knowledge be used to keep any knowledge from those who were deemed unworthy to receive it. Thus the lesson was learned that the proverbial keys to the kingdom always lie within one's grasp if they so desire. As for the Christ Consciousness, one had to reposition oneself to reach it.

Chapter 26 The Transition Of The Ages

In general, THE AQUARIAN GOSPEL OF JESUS THE CHRIST provided valuable insight into the meaning of the transition of the Ages. It was comparable in tone and presentation to the Gnostic gospels. Although it was received by an individual who had no knowledge of these gospels in his lifetime, the messages were remarkably compatible. This book put the life and teaching of the Christ into the context of the transition of the ages, Piscean to Aquarian. It also made clear the precession of the equinoxes was an opportunity for human growth at every level, intellectual, emotional, and spiritual. That indicated an evolutionary process had been engaged.

Each step in the energy cycle of the Ages represented a manifestation of divine purpose that guided the spiritual evolution of the human being as an individual and a race. No demarcation of wall-clock time could be rightly considered to be a boundary between Ages. Its significance pertained only to the fact that a human being lived on a biological clock. Such a time sequence was understandable to humankind, but it meant little or nothing in the reckoning of the cosmic timepiece. When conditions were ripe for it, evolution occurred. In the cosmic scheme of things, change occurred on a time clock of events like the procession of the equinoxes, or the life cycle of a star, or some other suitable manner for measuring the motion of celestial bodies. In the realm of substance and motion, cause and effect governed change. The causes for change were dependent more upon a timed sequence of events and the fulfillment of laws, than a date or mathematical calculation.

Before adopting the Aquarian Age directive, the individual must come to terms with the lessons of the Piscean Age. The consummating force of this Age was Yeshua the Christ whose expressed purpose was to show the way to Truth by his teachings and the example of his life. He said repeatedly, "*I am the way*", but for the most part humanity did not go that way. They may have intended to follow him, but historical records indicated they were intentionally led astray to satisfy the needs of ego for power and dominion.

As foretold in the biblical account of REVELATION, humanity was deceived by a band of power-seekers who usurped a righteous cause and invested it in the institutionalization of the earthly glory that was the empire of Rome. The home base of the Harlot and the Beast thus became the focal point of the faith, and when it ascended the throne, darkness fell. In an attempt to establish the Universal Church in a rejuvenated version of the new Holy Roman Empire, the power-seekers succeeded in undermining the message of Yeshua by reinvesting the process and principles of the Christ in an unholy marriage of Church and State. Throughout this age, Orthodox Christians regarded the man, Yeshua, as the end, forming a personality cult of gigantic proportions to preserve his identity among men. A fossilized messiah was put on exhibit, and it showed the way to ideological bondage. Thereafter a religious expression of universal faith called Catholicism capitalized upon the persona of the Christ and its saints by bastardizing their teachings, and parlayed it into a thousand basilicas filled with hundreds of thousands penitent kneelers. An auric identity was forged from the collective desires of the light-seekers which were but the shell of a man who embodied the Logos, the Anointed One. Subsequently it was perverted by the power-seekers into a spiritual monopoly to wield the power and influence of the Fathers of the Church, in whose stead corporal power was concentrated. They gave humanity a doctrine to observe which they wrapped around the enlightened teachings of the Christ. In essence they erected a magnificent lighthouse illuminating a sea of desert sands.

The true mandate of the continuing human experience was the revelation that Laws were conceived to effectuate a spiritual evolution enacted by an individual's free will. With cause and effect, the individual was shown that a perfect man was the consummation of life. Therefore the Eternal Wheel churned the human soul through the experience of karmic conflicts in the crucible of physical life until a perfect specimen was forged. The purification process operated within the Mind of the Deity directing its impulses through The Seven Laws of Creation: Order, Balance, Harmony, Growth, God-perception, Love, and Compassion. Impurities, carnal or astral, were purged by friction with true Virtue. Thus the cleansing fire produced a pure essence of mind within the vehicle of self, clear and unequivocal. Henceforth one was theoretically prepared for the next stage in human development, that of the next Age in sequence.

According to the sages, it was the duty of the son or daughter of man to express the five virtues that had been mandated with humanity's descension to flesh. The human virtues of Faith, Understanding, Justice, Hope, and Compassion, when sincerely felt and practiced within the full scope of human interaction generated a metamorphosis of the gross substance to the sublime, an expression of spiritual alchemy.

The purpose of the Aquarian Age, Yeshua's message, was to view the essence of life for what it was without the shadows of preconceived notions or prejudices clouding one's judgment. Stimulating others to seek a peaceful co-existence with Nature and among human beings was the method by which it could be achieved. Only in this way could humanity be deterred from its destructive impulses. These impulses were manifested in a disregard for Nature as a living being unto itself, disrespect for the sanctity of all life and how it was interconnected at every plane of existence, and an intense narcissism that disregarded the inalienable rights of any other human being, except oneself.

The next step in human evolution will feature the realization of the hidden potential of the human mind, and how to put the sibilant powers of insight and intuition to constructive use. With this knowledge, the son or daughter of man may transcend the limiting conditions of the flesh, and ascend to the true station as a son or daughter of Yahweh as the Essene foresaw. The accomplishment of this task was as easy or as difficult as one made it. For the unaware, it would require a total departure from their current lives because they did not respond to the Light at present. For the imposters, it will be a shock to their senses shattering all notions held near and dear to them that had been exposed as transparent when held up to the Light. For the enlightened few, it would be the fulfillment of an evolutionary mandate enacted when the Universe was but a formless void. For those who were prepared it was sure to lead to an eventual conclusion of a life within Spirit and an understanding of what it truly meant to be a son or daughter of Yahweh. For those who were not, it would herald the end of their world, and the beginning of their worst nightmare -- a world where all vestiges of materialism were rent asunder.

With the introduction of the Aquarian experience, humanity had yet another opportunity to right the wrongs of the past. While these errors could not be undone, errors in judgment could always be corrected in present time. There always existed a window of opportunity to do what was right as well as continue to do what was wrong. One always had the choice to take the right steps at the right time. If the will was there to take those steps, no one or thing could prevent one from taking them, not Yahweh, or any angel, demon, or another human being. One may be impressed to proceed in one direction or another and acquiesce to those influences, but the choice remained always with the individual. Such was the tone and tenor of Natural Law. Offered by the Aquarian Age was the challenge to all sons or daughters of men to take a quantum leap in their development to achieve what had been ordained to be the ultimate destiny of the human being.

The polarizing effects of the Canopy of Light that had enveloped Earth to raise the consciousness of all concerned will demarcate those who could accept Truth from those who could not. As the Light infiltrated every living thing, the essence of Spirit in each individual will be stimulated to move. Whether it will be felt as a stabilizing or de-stabilizing influence will depend upon how each individual recognized and reacted to the movement as they perceived it. Each from their own vantage point will decide in which direction to move. When one was bathed in the Light, all filters one had applied to block it will be stripped, all personality traits will evaporate, and all costumes worn will be shed. One's true character will be revealed. No longer will one be able to hide their motivations in the shadows. They will be apparent for all to see who was capable of seeing them. No prognostication of effect could alleviate individual responsibility because there was no escape from the consequence.

Once one became familiar with the teachings of THE CHILDREN OF THE LAW OF ONE, one understood how wise the Atlanteans were to preserve these teachings. Whenever Earth Changes were imminent, it was wise to put their preservation high on the list of priorities. Thoth made the effort to preserve them once before when he carried them to Egypt. As scribe for the gods, Thoth was credited with authorship of all the sacred books of the Egyptians. The hope was wise individuals were already making preparations to do the same. If it was appropriate to save anything for the rebirth of civilization, that was it.

Every human being had a stake in the concluding chapter of the Piscean Age, regardless of circumstance. The course of human events will necessitate a stance be taken, and a choice be made. Whether or not one believed in the legitimacy of this destiny, it mattered not. The course had been determined as the mechanism of the Universe continued its progression through the precession of the equinoxes. Once the wheels were set in motion, they could not be stopped. Through one may pause to take a breath or think a thought, time still moved forward a second at a time.

It was an undeniable fact that in the current age a rift existed between spiritualism and materialism. Over the ages, a duality had developed between satisfying the needs of body and soul. Primarily because conventional wisdom had always equated religion with spirituality, humanity anticipated that religious doctrine also equated to Universal Law. In so far as Webster's dictionary supported that misconception, religion had assumed the mantle of catering to the needs of the soul. But the fact was spiritualism and materialism was only opposite sides of the same coin. They came from the same Source. Since Universal Law had both physical and metaphysical components, by necessity human beings had a foot in both worlds. They saw the dichotomy, but viewed it as an effect of a preference for one or the other, and consequently had attempted to separate one from the other when no such division really existed. No wall could exist between them. They must collaborate or a physical world would not even exist. Furthermore the absence of physical manifestation would mean the metaphysical would exist as one thing where the parts were indistinguishable from each other. It was true human beings existed as separate entities, but they were also parts of the Whole, the One. The One subdivided itself so that individual souls could exist. It was also true human beings lived with a figment of imagination that set one apart from another so that a distinction could be made between separate consciousness and universal consciousness.

However if one believed the coin represented the One, the relationship between spiritualism and materialism was seen as collaborative, not in opposition. The rift must be straddled, meaning there was a point of reference where one side could communicate with the other. Plato believed that too, and it formed the base of his philosophical teachings. There was a symbiotic link between, the meaning of which was transparent to the beholder. That was why Hermetic philosophy coined the phrase, *as above, so below*. It was a concept embraced by Platonic philosophy as well. It represented the working formula of the connection between God, Man, and Nature, the Trinity of form and substance.

While it implied that each individual was striving to reunite with the One, the soul's lesson plans were individualized. Each individual learned what they needed to learn at the appointed time. The spiritual meaning of separate but equal taught that each individual learned the lessons it needed to learn at its own pace as well. But the way was blocked by the selfishness of the separate self. When the way was cleared, another door opened. When this happened it did so when that unit of soul was enlightened. It meant it recognized it was an individual which found its place within the One. Were it not for the prospect of enlightenment, no individual would ever find its way home. And the greatest a ccomplishment for any individual was to recognize Oneness while retaining recognition of his or her individuality. These individuals saw both the portal and panoramic views at the same moment in time, and understood that they were One.

    While it might not seem logical to the human mind that change operates on different economies of scale, the Universal Mind understood that logic. That mattered more than what any human being thought. If one was to understand the true import of the *as above, so below* philosophy, this made perfect sense. Generally the uninitiated did not see things as they were at a macrocosmic level. Normally one was bearing witness to their own narrow, portal view of how change affected them. That outlook was a slice of life that cut across the grain and provided a cross-sectional view. While the portal view was the view an individual had, the top view was the panoramic view from the Universal Mind. That was the big picture of all the parts of the One Thing. Until one achieved enlightenment, one did not partake of that panoramic view. It was difficult to fathom what that actually meant for one who had always seen the world through that portal. Nonetheless it was what it was. If one saw things as disjointed and separated, reality will be viewed that way. However if one saw things as connected and interrelated, reality will be viewed that way instead. But again only an enlightened being could see it in the fullness of the interrelated moving parts and their relationships. Hence one only saw with clarity what the conscious mind could draw associations to. That was to say one could only view the cause-and-effect relationship of the connection, rather than the underlying causation. The fault rested only in not wanting to expand the view to encompass the Universal Mind, that which was the source of causation.

    The panoramic view yielded an entirely different image from the portal view. Because human perception was made to serve the will of the portal views, selfishness ruled the world and everything in it. Achieving salvation would not only entail a revamping of our philosophical and economic ways and means at their most fundamental level, but would also include a re-examination of our belief systems and philosophies to readjust our views of God, humanity, and Nature. This was all that a man or woman of true spiritual import could ever hope for. But the question remained: will reason prevail or will a dogged determination to preserve an imprudent ideology preside over our ultimate demise? Only the practice of agape on a global scale enabled the salvation of the race. But it was a door humanity must choose to walk through together. It has never been any different nor will it ever be. Choice was the rule, rather than the exception to it. Humanity must recognize that observing any ideology must not preempt the health and welfare of humanity at large. The Will of the Universal Mind took precedence over human beliefs of what was best for humanity and the natural world. But the course of human events was chosen rather than mandated. Thus a lifeline tossed to the drowning man could pull him to safety or provide enough rope for him to hang himself before he was dragged to shore. It was all in how that lifeline was used.

The annals of THE CHILDREN OF THE LAW OF ONE were an

open book provided one understood the language. Anyone was capable of reading it, but to understand it, one had to be one open to the process they employed. Unfortunately most individuals had been stunted in their growth. Apparently, they never learned to question: why not? Where the fault lies was a matter of debate. But often one opened the doors they chose to open, and left those closed they chose to leave closed. Whether fear or negligence was the culprit, there was no good reason to fear. As for negligence, that was an individual choice. An individual chose it or was advised to choose it. In either scenario fear or negligence were tools used to keep one from attaining knowledge. Those that used it equated imagination with fancy and considered insight and intuition to be inferior to reason.

In many ways the free-thinkers who thought outside-of-the-box posed a danger to those straight-laced thinkers whose thinking was limited to the dimensions of their box. Consequently the Children of Belial who the Essene termed *the world of divine anger* strove to keep a lid on that box. Such had been their objective throughout recorded history – stilling the inquiring mind. The word history literally meant *his story*, but it was not a single individual's property. It belonged to all human beings. An individual was entitled to find their own place in it. To decode it one started by feeling their way through their internal dialogue.

However, one reached the concluding chapter of their lives whether or not they were prepared for it, or had the answers to the questions they had been asking for the greater part of their lives. One had no choice but to be satisfied with that. Suffice it to say life was not fair, but reality always found a way to creep in. One must be prepared for the end regardless of when it arrived.

Dying was easier than living. One had only to endure pain for a definable period of time. It was living that was hard. Conceivably one's pain could last a lifetime. If one was to serve as a model, was not a perfect life the greater achievement? Was not perfecting the execution of it the greater chore? Furthermore its accomplishment was not even possible except it be fully vested on one's own terms and conditions, and only if they be consistent with the Law of One. The reclamation project of the human being began with striving to live a virtuous life. The time-honored way to do so was by acquiring the knowledge which permitted one to know the difference between virtue and vice. And one could not know either without knowing both.

Their entire teaching of the Law of One could be boiled down into one commandment. It was one everyone knew. Many had referred to it over the years as the Golden Rule, and it probably had the distinction of being the commandment that had been broken the most. Perhaps the correct terminology was it was the one commandme nt that was never obeyed. It was the single commandment Yeshua gave to his disciples that bore repeating. He said, *"Thou shalt love the lord thy God with all thy heart, and with all thy soul, and with all thy mind. This is the first and great commandment. And the second is like unto it, Thou shalt love thy neighbour as thyself. On these two commandments hang all the law and the prophets." (Matthew 22:37-40)*.

If one equated the term *God* to *Self* like Thoth did within the as above, so below methodology, then that means that *IT* was equal to *you*. Thus you were commanded to love yourself, and love your neighbor as much as you love yourself. If you obeyed this commandment with the fervor and resolve that you committed to observing your ideology, there would already be a paradise on Earth. If you failed to do so, the opposite was true. And that negative experience which humanity shared at present where a man loved neither himself nor his neighbor was because of the free will to follow the dictates of ego. The circumstances revealed an intense dissatisfaction with self, where it was going, and what it had become in the process. With any experiment, the calamity would be repeated until the lesson was learned, because after all that was what life was all about. It was hit or miss. Sometimes the experiment went smoothly, and sometimes it went haywire. But in either case effort was required to make it happen, whether it be a success or a failure. And no one knew the outcome beforehand no matter what they thought they knew.

To play it by ear seemed to be the message relayed, a bit simplistic but accurate if accomplished with the correct frame of mind. In a Universe where choice was the rule, and free will and cause and effect reigned supreme, there was little else to do but to make the correct choices, and go with the flow. Despite what the theists had to say, the Almighty made it that way. Human beings could do little more than obey the Christ's one commandment to love unconditionally and live their lives accordingly. In other words, the gauntlet thrown down before you was to be the best person one could be without qualification. Once one picked it up, as Thoth suggested, *"now the miracles begin"*. The connection was made. The path was laid. Destiny was fulfilled.

Chapter 27 Conclusion

Living your life in accordance with The Bible made perfect sense until you realized it was written at a time when women were the property of men, slavery was commonplace, and human trafficking was rampant. In those days, death was the penalty for even minor offenses because compassion was in short supply, and the rule of law pertained primarily to religious Law. Certainly it was not humanity's finest hour. It was a time when belief in gods and magic was the order of the day, and the works of the gods were used to explain every unknown which included almost everything. It was also a time when adult men knew less about the world around them than the average middle school student did today. In this context, the Bible made perfect sense in the historical time frame in which it was written, but those days were long gone and forgotten, or were they?

At this juncture, the operative question should be asked – why did religious movements desire to take humanity back to that time? The goal of the opposing crusades of both Christian Evangelism and Muslim Jihad was to bring back the past when the gods commanded and the faithful obeyed. It was a time when if one had faith, no thinking was required because the path was laid out for them. There was no need to question the answers provided in Scripture because it was believed God put them there, and endorsed them wholeheartedly. It was not recognized then that God had no need of Scripture written by human beings. It was only Man who needed Scripture, but men failed to acknowledge it. The theists even pretended that God inspired its writing because they depended upon it to answer their own questions. They referred to it often because that was the intentional limit of their knowledge and experience.

In The Silence, a man heard an inner voice, and he did not recognize it as his own. He thought it was God or The Adversary, and depending upon the content of the conversation acted accordingly. However, he did not trust his own intuition and dictates of his Conscience to determine good from evil. He depended upon the voices in his head or the words written in Scripture to show the way. Furthermore he compounded that error by measuring his progress by the successes or failures in his life to follow its advice.

After the introduction of Tom Paine's RIGHTS OF MAN and AGE OF REASON, an individual's Voice became prominent. It became the individual's choice whether to stagnate or grow. You could ascend the steps to sit at the right hand of God or you could kneel at his feet and be at the mercy of his every whim like HE was king and you were the servant. Yeshua had shown the way by preaching unconditional love for each of God's creatures, but churches, temples, and mosques in large part (as elucidated in the preceding text) did not relay this message to their constituents. They chose instead to preach loyalty, reverence, and obedience to Authority instead. An Authority that declared itself to be lord and master of humanity, the sovereignty that never ends, amen, and humanity was just supposed to accept it.

That Authority established religions that observed a parent-child relationship between God and Man (as declared in The Nicene Creed), but left no provision in it for human beings to grow up. That was the crux of the problem. Unlike the processes of the Natural World, there was no opportunity for human beings to grow and evolve. This was contrary to the material and spiritual expression of the Seven Principles of Creative Force in the Universe. As noted repeatedly in the text of this manuscript, they were Order, Balance, Harmony, Growth, God-perception, Love, and Compassion. Each living thing abided at the nexus of the Consummate Force and Infinite Intelligence of the Triune God.

If you think God created Man so that he could be a servant-in-waiting, then you have resigned yourself to that fate. Or you could aspire to what Yeshua wanted all human beings to be: full partners in creating a world where peace, love, and brotherhood reigned via immersion into the Christ Consciousness. This notion was designed to supersede a world where all human intercourse was overseen by gods, kings, and their egomaniacal needs and desires. In other words, all human beings would eventually ascend to the station of being a Christ themselves, in essence, mature spiritually and emotionally. That was the mission and overriding purpose of Yeshua's life, rather than to sacrifice his life to 'wash away the sins of the world'. The mission was to raise the consciousness of humanity at large, one soul at time, to occupy the place where he sat, in the mind and heart. He in as much said so precisely in the Gospel of John (14:12-14) as already cited in the text. At present we were a long way from that happening on Earth, but Yeshua had hope it would be accomplished in time.

In the aftermath of completing this expose on the Christian faith of our forefathers, what I found intriguing about interrogating the works of God was not to challenge HIS existence but HIS motivation. Considering HIS existence, I asked myself in all sincerity: was God a HE, a SHE or an IT or none of the above? I could not fathom which it would be. Perhaps it did not matter at all, but using the masculine form of pronoun to represent God seemed to be the default usage. You could blame that assignment on the Nicene Creed which made the claim that God was the Father, and the Gospels which reinforced that notion. Surely it was an everlasting tribute to living in a patriarchic society. No offense was really intended to alternative assignments of gender to a Supreme Being whose existence defied the very assignment of a gender. I supposed the correct assignment would be to say that God was all genders since being designated the All-in-All like the Essene, Gnostics, and Children of the Law of One did.

While considering HIS motivation, one looked at Creation in its splendor and variety. The appropriate response to me seemed to be: why do it at all? What was the reason for it? It would require quite an effort to accomplish this feat. This was what I wondered about. Why go through with the effort? The return on investment for the Almighty seemed to be a little less than it should be. The reason of it went to motivation. What motivated God to be the Creator of all things material and immaterial? I found it an appropriate question to ask, but the Silence provided no answer.

Nonetheless I have not a clue what to say any more

about God, prayer or love. I was all too consumed about my opinions on things to allow God to get a word in edgewise. It was an issue for the Ages, but the explanation was above my pay grade. Therefore I will let the words of St Thomas Aquinas stand for mine on such matters. Concerning the nature of God he said, *"It is necessary to posit something which is necessary of itself, and has no cause of its necessity outside of itself, but is the cause of necessity in other things. And all people call this thing God."* Thus it would appear God was the stimulus that moved thought, word, and deed via conscious, subconscious and unconscious repetitive motion. The keyword here was 'necessity', as if the universe could not exist without it. I supposed that would be the definitive statement concerning the existence of God.

    St Thomas Aquinas was a proponent of Aristotelian logic. Therefore he adhered to a system of reasoning that focused on syllogism. That was a three-step agreement of conditional, categorical and disjunctive reasoning used to reach a logical conclusion. It followed that God was Aristotle's prime mover plus the Judeo-Christian equivalent of the penultimate Father Confessor according to the Nicene Creed. God, being the source of causation of all things as well as the effect of that causation made God rightfully so the alpha and the omega, the beginning and the ending, at the same moment in time, for all time.

Regarding prayer St Thomas Aquinas continued, "*It is clear that he does not pray, who, far from uplifting himself to God, requires that God shall lower Himself to him and who resorts to prayer to stir the man in us to will what God wills, but only to persuade God to will what the man in us wills.*" Thus primarily the penitent kneeler served himself or herself while pretending to serve God. Only the petulant pious it would seem required contrition when their needs were not met. Apparently, the reason for prayer was the determining factor between selfishness and selflessness. However was not prayer a form of meditation from which thought was absent by design? Therefore it lacked the cause-and-effect relationship that spurred action, and consequently also the motivation that accompanied it. Hence it was a perfect form of prayer whereby the one who meditated made no request. One only endeavored to align oneself with the spiritual pulse of the Universe, and flow with it. Thus meditation was a selfless form of prayer.

And he ended by saying, "*Love must precede hatred, and nothing is hated save through being contrary to a suitable thing which is loved. And hence it is that every hatred is caused by love.*" That was the quintessential statement of love's cause and effect relationship when twisted into the myriads of shapes it took when affected by human emotion. And if one still wondered why some of the most heinous crimes in human history had been caused by the most pious individuals, the preceding statement explained why. Hence the practice of cultism was the bane of humanity, not its saving grace.

On the Mount of Olives, Yeshua stated he had not come to abolish but to fulfill the Law of Moses. That meant his objective was to tie up the loose ends of all the prophecy of the prophets that had come before him; he being the crowning achievement of what went before him. In the Sermon on the Mount, Yeshua encapsulated the essential teaching of Christianity. That teaching, called The Beatitudes as recorded in (Matthew 5:3-12), was as follows: *Blessed are the poor in spirit: for theirs is the kingdom of heaven. Blessed are they that mourn: for they shall be comforted. Blessed are the meek: for they shall inherit the earth. Blessed are they which do hunger and thirst after righteousness: for they shall be filled. Blessed are the merciful: for they shall obtain mercy. Blessed are the pure in heart: for they shall see God. Blessed are the peacemakers: for they shall be called the children of God. Blessed are they which are persecuted for righteousness' sake: for theirs is the kingdom of heaven. Blessed are ye, when men shall revile you, and persecute you, and shall say all manner of evil against you falsely, for my sake. Rejoice, and be exceeding glad: for great is your reward in heaven: for so persecuted they the prophets which were before you.*

The Beatitudes spoken by Yeshua in the Sermon on the Mount were the very core of Christian teaching. The number of Beatitudes was not significant. What was significant was the message of conciliation, compassion and agape they encompassed. Truly it was the voice of the Christ preserved for posterity. Furthermore the final statement reinforced the notion that Yeshua believed he was the culmination of the prophets and the summation of their message to humankind.

As for the Evangelicals, it was noteworthy that we did not hear them proclaim the significance of the message of the Beatitudes on a daily basis, but instead they promoted the Ten Commandments continually, and insisted they be posted on every school wall in the USA. However, it should be the Beatitudes that should be posted in their place because that was the true message of Christian teaching.

The fact that its importance in the dogma was often overlooked by modern Theists was truly disconcerting. It was one that the giver would want to be paid forward to all humankind for all time. With all due respect to Moses, for my part, it was the Beatitudes that should be put front and center in the human heart. That was because it was a message of positivism, rather than the underlying negativism of the dos and don'ts of the Ten Commandments. I truly believed Yeshua would want the same.

Furthermore since the Christ repeatedly said his followers could call him by name and he would be there, they anticipated it. *"For where two or three are gathered together in my name, there I am in the midst of them" (Matthew 18:20).* Unfortunately for millennia his followers had been invoking the name *Jesus* in their moments of desperation when their trials and tribulations peaked. Since the prophet's given name was Yeshua, would he respond? This was what I wondered about. Was it a call that went unanswered?

Chapter 28 Monolog

Because of the juncture at which I am left after writing this book, the research leads me to the following conclusions. They are the sum total of all the moving parts of the argument. It is where to go from here. From beginning to end, the salient question is: how has faith moved me if at all and to where have I been moved? The best answer to this question I can formulate follows as the quintessential statement of a child of the Law of One. It can be considered a replacement for the Nicene Creed, a statement that comes from the source of Infinite Intelligence, and stands as a testament of doctrine. I call it the *Declaration of the Son of Man*. It follows in its entirety.

HE WHO HAS NO NAME creates, destroys, and preserves ITS Creation complying with the precepts of the Law of One. From a universal perspective, creation and destruction are but singular events joined by the stabilizing influence of a preserving Nature. The harmonious continuity of the Creative Cycle of Life denotes a purpose both singular and plural that engineers a manifestation through the application of Universal Law. Toward this end, the evolutionary processes of body and soul were mandated to fulfill the need for Growth, and laboratories like Earth were created where that growth could occur. The world was created to be a proving ground for virtue where each individual tests his or her mettle in the crucible of material existence.

Virtue is described by the relative purity of one's mind. It determines the performance of the instruction achieved through the mental and emotional discipline over the inebriate of selfishness. Inevitably human actions and reactions will exalt or pervert the instructions transcribed within. But it is made to be an arduous process when one fails to abide by the precepts of Universal Law. Respect for the individual should replace a reliance on Piety because a respect for Virtue will naturally evolve from it. The attainment of a virtuous state of being is the one Ideal that needs to be maintained in the Society of Man. Its enactment is the completion of the self-divine. The objective is to grow beyond any self-imposed limitations, with the goal being ultimately, a perfection of self.

However before that can be accomplished, each individual must know his or her microcosmic universe completely, and express that knowledge with each breath. As one begins to understand how to separate Truth from fantasy, derive from it a Faith that comprehends the difference, one can deliver a compassionate Justice to all who seek it. Only when one learns the art of selflessness, can the promise of peace, justice, and the brotherhood of Man be realized. In this way only can knowledge be truly enacted; for the knowledge issued forth by the raving of the ego is truly a seed sown among thorns.

When the divine self is brought forth as the Christ suggested actions will be tempered with Compassion, thoughts will be founded upon Truth, and words will be bolstered by Faith. Once expressed, what was lacking in self will be replaced by the desire to achieve a fuller expression, and the willful persistence to accomplish it. When the divine self is neglected, it is forgotten. Therefore one must remember his or her divinity because this realization is the only avenue to freedom. Without it, the karmic wheel spins eternal, generating countless lifetimes of toil and travail. Spiritual evolution requires an effort from within to continuously improve, and carries with it an obligation of providing aid and comfort to one's fellow man. To abolish selfishness one must change the motive for material pursuits, by striving to be just, individual-to-individual. If one is ever to gain, one must not fear to lose an advantage. However if one fails to put aside his or her egomania, one can never be satisfied with oneself, with what is offered, or with what is gained. The perverse passion of interpersonal relationships can be turned to joy when the effort is made to give instead of take.

Many try to force a natural evolutionary process, that of becoming, because their impatience forces unnatural conclusions. Because they have not grasped the truth about Universal Law, many are talking when they should be listening, and acting compulsively to fulfill their obsessions. Silence, not debate, is the threshold to wisdom. Within one's own being are all of the answers worth knowing, but few realize it. They cannot wait for it to unfold naturally. They must unfold it by force. Most are constantly casting into the depths of uncharted waters attempting to find what lies close to the surface. They are unable to see beyond the scum that clouds the surface, and thus the pure waters beneath remain untapped.

To assemble the mosaic of humanity into a coherent whole is the goal of the All-in-All. It has charged each individual soul with a need to accomplish this feat. As each feels the urge to unite, he or she remembers the directive that has been encoded. Until that need can be brought forth into consciousness, no individual realizes why he or she has been placed here. Until realized the need resides in the recesses of the individual subconscious awaiting the moment of recognition like a seed waits for the warmth of the sun before it can grow. When it is touched by the Light and nourished by the water of life, the process of growth begins. No growth can occur in the vacuum of time and space. It requires the diversity of human circumstance and the fertile soil of material existence to take root. Truly human beings must find it within themselves to do the right thing at the right time for the right reason. And depend upon nothing other than one's native intuition and Conscience to advise one to do so. The transition from son or daughter of man to son or daughter of Yahweh is an open invitation to all individuals to experience without the coercion of institutionalization, but each chooses whether to be enslaved or free.

  Faith should not be subjected to the weights and measures of three-dimensional space, but rather tested in the pure waters of the soul. Strength of faith is determined by the seriousness of conviction to the Truth. Balance is a prime component of the Law because what is given is received in equal measure. However, when thoughts are enriched with virtue, exponential gains can be realized. The reiteration of virtuous thoughts produces virtuous deeds which as they enumerate constitute a virtuous life. The continuance of virtuous living is the express lane to a paradise on Earth. And when humanity joins in the spirit of Harmony and free will, all societal crises, divisive economic issues, racial injustices, and religious conflicts will be realized to be inconsequential because spiritual equality overrides all human conditions.

This is the one lesson which the Declaration of Independence attempts to relay which humanity in its blind allegiance to political one-upmanship fails to recognize. In the ace of those who seek to divide humanity, unity can be forged in spite of the efforts, they who foster all expression of political and societal enmity for their own again, expend to divide and conquer. As long as humanity continues down the path of conflict and disharmony, they revel in a job well done to preserve their cherished fiefdoms. Whether or not the purveyors of dissension and discord fully realize it, they have an equal share in the failure to unite humanity in a common cause under the auspices of Universal Law. Odds are that those who do not submit to Universal Law do not understand it. They may labor under the misconception that striving for balance and harmony is not a divine mandate. While equality, fraternity, and justice are man-made jurisdictions, they do spring from Universal Law to promote harmony in human relations.

Love alone is not enough to reach the heights of spiritual expression. Unless that Love is directed by the union of Force and Intelligence, it becomes the aimless romanticism of the simple-minded. The eloquent expression of the Triune God (Force, Intelligence, and Love), cannot be expressed by the simpleton who must be told what to believe. It can only be expressed by one who has mastered his or her Gnosis (knowledge) of self and God, realizing it is ONE. Truly it is the wise man or woman who does not worship at the temple of another, but instead purifies the temple of his or herself to be a fitting receptacle for the God within. Since God is the acknowledged source of the spiritual DNA all living beings carry, one can rightly say that God is the Father. But the equation of spiritual life cannot yield a product without a unification of the masculine and feminine principles within the matrix materialized by spiritual force. It is provoked by the catalyst of Love. The true Trinity of masculine principle, feminine principle and transcendent Spirit is expressed in the embodiment of body, mind, and soul united as ONE. Hence the relationship engenders spirit-in-flesh, and the transition from son or daughter of man to son or daughter of God is the realization. There is but One Thing from which all manifestation springs.

Humanity's greatest failing is the assumption that Truth can be mandated by faith, justice can be legislated by judicial decree, and compassion can be enforced by human institutions. The ultimate success of human endeavors operates from the inside out, rather than from the outside in, and from the bottom up rather than the top down. When one comes to the realization that the onus is upon each individual to be the manager of one's own life, then one's thinking is aligned with the natural course of human events. Of one's own volition, an individual must feel the urgency to perform to the pinnacle of one's ability for there to be everlasting success in any endeavor. The sooner one adapts one's thinking to preserving Universal Law, relinquishes the futile attempts to make it, and realizes the individual's role is only to interpret it, the more fortuitous his or her journey promises to be. To make the world a better place in which to live, each individual must be engaged in the spirit of free will, and reconcile one human heart at a time, starting with oneself. There is no pot of gold at the end of the rainbow, lest one put it there. It essentially means one reaps what one sows. Be satisfied with the fruit of one's labor. It is all one is owed.

In the final analysis, it will be discovered that the divine consciousness you have been invoking for aid and comfort all of your life is actually the divine part of you. You have simply failed to recognize this because your attention is focused upon the grandest of ideas, not the simplest. The simple truth can be the most elusive truth of all. It is easy to overlook the minute details when one is contemplating the intricacies of a grand design. When one has been instructed to dream the impossible dream, anything less than that seems mundane, unthinkable. Your task is to become the best you it is possible for you to be, nothing more. It is far better to live each day for itself than to abide by an expectation of things to come that may never come to pass. Revelation is too much to expect when one cannot follow the simplest of instructions; that is for individuals to love one another unconditionally, without reservation. In actuality, no further revelation is necessary; for the door to eternity will be opened wide when one accedes to the Christ's request. Otherwise it will be shut tight; for love lubricates the hinges, while hate causes them to rust. The value of any revelation achieved in the absence of the Master's prime directive is thereby diminished. If one cannot accept his message of selfless service and compassion for one's fellow man on its own merits, then one has not heard the message. If one does not do everything in one's power to incorporate it into every waking minute of one's life, then all further acts are futile. How much more simple can it be? If one chooses to be selfish instead of selfless, it merely proves one does not understand the message.

    Herein lay the ambivalent meaning of the simple truth: it

is what it is, but it is what you make of it. The way it is, is the way it is supposed to be. One cannot prove other wise, and should not devote any energy to do so. In the end you are measured by how much you love, as well as by how much you are loved. There is little else one can do to secure a place in paradise, but earn one's way by placing virtue before all other achievements.

One can be assured no one is keeping any scorecard that is binding, except your internal auditor that records every move you make as a matter of record. Your code of conduct is self-regulatory. Not abiding by the dictates of Conscience is your own cross to bear. Certainly no one can carry it for you, nor would that meet your need. It is the epitome of blind ignorance to believe that you will ever stop learning and growing. No one can open up a book, and point the truth out to you. The living truth you discover yourself by living the simple truth. Only you know when you have found it, and only you can actuate it for yourself. Truly it is the most personal of revelations.

Even a realized being must continue to evolve on a

designated pathway. Because a complete understanding of the Creative Cycle of Life is probably beyond the scope of human comprehension, the individual may imagine that Life has an end, but these speculations are a result of limited insight. While human existence has a beginning and an end, the life of the soul is neither on a time clock, nor is it limited to a space of four dimensions. Having no discernible beginning or end, it exists extemporaneously. It needs no reason nor relies upon faith, and understanding its agenda is beyond the scope of human capability. It exists even without an acknowledgement of its existence.

Thus the fog of human miscomprehension clears when one makes the effort to resolve the rumor and innuendo that inevitably accompanies the quest for knowledge. One should not merely assume one's association with the conceited truth-tellers of ideology guarantees enlightenment. More likely the opposite is true; for their ulterior motives are too often masked by feigned sincerity. No foregone conclusions substitute for the Truth because it is an acquired taste. It pre-exists the human need to know it, and would exist even if no human being existed to believe in it. Understanding the objectivity of Universal Law can be circumvented by one's portal view. Therefore to realize it one must see it from God's perspective rather than one's own. After one has purged all vestiges of self-interest from one's agenda, one's view is refocused. It is the view from the God Within.

Embrace your experience whatever it is, you worked hard to earn it. But realize you owe allegiance to yourself only. Your experience helps make you who you are and your only choice in the matter is to embrace it or deny it. It will not change who you are, but it will set the stage for how it will be manifested. Your life is guaranteed to be a mixed bag of pleasure and pain, but it is no more one than the other. It only seems so as desired by those who strive for an advantage. If you fear your pain, it will destroy you. Thus you must em brace it to rob it of the chance to hold dominion over you. When you can, you are poised to carve out a destiny. Only then can you say you truly lived. Until then you merely occupied space.

The principles of secular humanism stand alone as

the absolute testament to the merit of the Golden Rule. Without the trappings of human ideology, the fatherhood of God and the brotherhood of Man are given expression. Their driving force is to live in accordance with Universal Law. Love does not insist upon its own way. It is only personal bias that demands compliance. Only the obsessive-com pulsive personality demands that everyone else follows his or her rules. The All-in-All does not demand it. IT does not have to because Universal Law makes life unfold naturally. It is inherent in the system. It is a natural outcome if one has the foresight and willingness to make the correct choices. It is one's duty to recognize this, and act accordingly.

In accordance with the Law, your sole responsibility is to connect to the One within you. Within you, the messiah awaits. You venture inward to latch onto it instead of reaching outward to gather it in. In essence the proposition is to strive to be more spiritual and less materialistic. A connection to the higher mind is enabled by a re-establishment of the chain of command. Know that an untapped resource is no resource at all.

If you follow the dictates of your higher mind, you cannot take a wrong turn. That is the answer you seek. There is no other to impart that is of value. Thus we revisit the topic of purpose to declare you must find it within yourself. No one else can give it to you, nor would you want anyone to. It is your obligation to know what it is and go with it. It is incumbent upon you to choose wisely. Be advised that if you think you have to join a religious cult to find yourself, think again. No joining is required. If you need to join something to be complete, then there is something you lack in yourself that no 'joining' to religious cults can provide.

Remember no principle is worth espousing if in order to uphold it you have to hurt the one you love. Let compassion reign, lest one's endeavors be perverted by self-interest. Let love radiate through one's motivations, lest one's character be stained with self-centeredness. Where the love-light leads, others are certain to follow.

Knowing is not an end in itself. Doing is its end. To seek is not enough, but it is a valid beginning. Finding initiates a second beginning, and when it is no longer enough to know, it becomes time to effectuate.

Chapter 29 Epilog

Ultimately when it comes to the here and now, religion is the issue, specifically the balance between faith and reason. In the human quest for Gnosis, it gets in the way. Rather than waiting for God to express an opinion in the manner that suits HIM, it endeavors to speak for HIM. In the Silence, Faith assumes too much, and reasons too little. Belief is a human proposition. Would God exist even if there was no one to believe in HIM? That is the salient question, and the real issue is: did God create Man or did Man create God? To this day, no one can come up with an adequate answer to these questions, no matter how hard they try because no proof is at hand. Again the Silence is deafening.

Theists assume religion activates divine rights to worship at the throne of one's choosing that preclude all human rights. That includes the right to be free, the right to believe in what one wishes, and the right to live the life one desires the way one desires to live it. These desires encompass free will and self-determination. Per Thomas Paine, they are the core of all human rights. All of which indicates one should have the God-given right to exist independent of church doctrine. By definition, religious freedom is freedom from religion as much as it is freedom of religion. Be assured that is how the Founders saw it. However no theist sees it quite that way. They see their way as the only way, the residue of a gift of Grace. Thus it confirms that religious faith represents the omniscience of selfishness as much as it could be considered the healing balm of personal salvation. This healing balm they consider to be a gift from God for having faith, as well as a by-product of their faith.

A tendency toward Christo fascism abides in the heart of the Evangelist, and it is revealed in an intense desire to love God which abdicates any sense of rationality. In point of fact they consider all human beings to be sinners that require saving, in spite of the fact no theist has the god given right to make this diagnosis or provide this resolution. This ultimately leads the faithful to having a perverted sense of being my brother's keeper.

To the masses, Evangelicals are currently marketing a prosperity gospel in which Yeshua would not even recognize his place in it. What the theists do not seem to realize is that the prosperity gospel is only profitable for the ones who sell it. Buyers must beware. The predictions of the Book of REVELATION have come to pass, but this time no one will return to cast the moneychangers out of the Temple. The sons and daughters of men are left to their own devices on how to deal with the situation, as it should be.

If there truly is a Deity to worship and IT is the creator of all things corporal and spiritual, IT would be wise enough not to make adherence to church doctrine a hard fast requirement for sentient beings. Moreover there is no reason to believe that a supreme being would even require church membership. Those would be human requirements to set up the church to be the intermediary between God and Man. Infinite Intelligence does not require such a relationship be maintained, only humans do between each other. Therefore stop pretending that God or Yeshua commanded the creation of the Universal Church because it makes no sense that either would. The *church* of which they spoke was the temple of the living spirit, the human body, rather than a building. They desired Man to preserve and honor that structure instead, and the Earth which provides a residence for it. No one needs a building to worship God in, unless the purpose for having one is to put a price on the practice of faith.

The perfect rationale to pursue an understanding of Faith, however, is a statement attributed to St Anselm: *"I do not seek to understand in order that I may believe, but I believe in order to understand"*. This statement reveals an open-minded approach to the greatest of questions – does God exist or am I being deceived? I do not claim to possess all the answers but I demand the right to pursue the course of action in finding them that I choose. I am fully prepared to accept responsibility for my own actions. Therefore the optimal conclusion to reach is that each of us is our own savior, and that each of us are free to pursue the course we choose to accomplish it.

In confronting the theists, I would say this: In all honesty, my purpose is not to insult your religious beliefs. It is instead to point out the error of your ways with dispassionate logic. I am merely trying to explain why those beliefs cannot be true as you believe them. They do not follow logically. It is not that you cannot have beliefs, but that you are not permitted to force others to have the same ones you do. Then they compound the error by saying it was so ordained by God. In substance, your error is legislating conformity to a personal opinion rather than an eternal truth. I will leave it at that, and end this dissertation. You go your way and I'll go mine, secure in the knowledge that it is precisely the way Infinite Intelligence wants it to be: to each its own.

BIBLIOGRAPHY

1. The Gospel of Matthew; King James Version of the New Testament; text references appear in chapter 1 "Argument" on page 17 and chapter 15 "Politics of Power" on page 143 for verse 16: 18-19; in chapter 6 "Biblical Sleight of Hand" pp 52-53 for verse 2: 16; in chapter 6 "Biblical Sleight of Hand" on pp 55-56 for verse 3: 13-17; in chapter 8 "Nag Hammadi Library" on page 79 for verse 21: 10-13 and chapter 22 "Mission of Yeshua" on pp 220-221 for verse 10: 34-39; in chapter 26 "Transition of the Ages" on page 281 for verse 22: 37-40; in chapter 27 "Conclusion" on pp 290-291 for verse 5:3-12; in chapter 27 "Conclusion" on page 292 for verse 18: 20

2. The Jewish War and Antiquities of the Jews; author: Flavius Josephus; book identification and text references appear in chapter 3 "Man, Yeshua" on pp 28-30

3. The Life of Apollonius of Tyana; author: Philostratus the Elder; Harvard University Press 2005; book identification appear in chapter 4 "Man, Apollonius" on pp 35-37

4. Did Jesus Exist? The Historical Argument for Jesus of Nazareth; Author: Bart D. Ehrman; Harper Collins USA 2012; ISBN 978-006-2204608; book identification and text references appear in chapter 4 "Man, Apollonius" on pp 37-38

5. The Works of Philo; author Philo Judaeus of Alexandria; discourse: On the Contemplative Life or Supplicants; Hendrickson Publishers LLC UK 1993; ISBN 978-156563-80909; book identification and text references appear in chapter 5 "Philo of Alexandria" on pp 47-50

6. The Gospel of Luke; English Standard version of the New Testament; text references appear in chapter 6 "Biblical Sleight of Hand" on page 54 for verse 2: 46-49

7. The Gospel of John; King James Version of the New Testament; text references appear in chapter 6 "Biblical Sleight of Hand" on p 59 for verse 14:12-14; in chapter 19 "Battleground of

Doctrine" on page 185 for verse 20: 29

8. The Complete Dead Sea Scrolls in English; edited by Geza Vermes, author, translator; Allen Lane; The Penguin Press UK 1997; ISBN 978-0713-991314; for book identification: in chapter 1 "Argument"; in chapter 4 "Man, Apollonius"; in chapter 7 "Essene"; in chapter 9 "Descent to Untruth"; in chapter 10 "Issue of Gnosis"; in chapter 13 "Role of Women in Gnosticism"; in chapter 23 "Children of the Law of One"

9. The Book of Genesis; King James Version of the Old Testament; text references appear in chapter 13 "Role of Women in Gnosticism" on pp 123-124 for verse 2: 7; in chapter 16 "Nicene Creed" on page 157 for verse 5: 21-24

10. The Acts of the Apostles; King James Version of the New Testament; for book identification: in chapter 9 "Descent to Untruth"; in chapter 10 "Issue of Gnosis"; in chapter 12 "Sin and Absolution", and in chapter 16 "Nicene Creed"; text reference in chapter 8 "Nag Hammadi Library" on page 80 for On the Road to Damascus and in chapter 12 "Sin and Absolution" on page 116 for the Pentecost

11. The Book of Revelation; King James Version of the New Testament; for book identification: in chapter 7 "Essene"; in chapter 8 "Nag Hammadi Library"; in chapter 16 "Nicene Creed"; in chapter 22 "Mission of Yeshua"; in chapter 23 "Children of the Law of One"; in chapter 26 "The Transition of the Ages"; in chapter 29 "Epilog"

12. The Gnostic Gospels; author Elaine Pagels; Vintage Books, Random House; New York USA 1979; ISBN 978-0679-724532

13. The Nag Hammadi Library; edited by James M. Robinson; San Francisco USA 1977; for book identification: in chapter 1 "Argument"; in chapter 4 "Man, Apollonius"; in chapter 8 "Nag Hammadi Library"; in chapter 9 "Descent to Untruth"; in chapter 10 "Issue of Gnosis"; in chapter 17 "Monophysitism"; in chapter 18 "Gnostics in the Crosshairs"; in chapter 21 "Christ, The Traveler"; in chapter 22 "Mission of Yeshua"; text references appear in

chapter 10 "Issue of Gnosis" on page 92 for Gnostic Gospel, The Origin of the World; in chapter 10 "Issue of Gnosis" on page 93 for Gnostic Gospel, Philosophumenia; in chapter 10 "Issue of Gnosis" on pp 96-98 for Gnostic Gospel, Vision of Poimandres; in chapter 11 "Descent to Untruth" on pp 104-105 for Gnostic Gospel, The Testimony of Truth; in chapter 12 "Sin and Absolution" on pp 117-118 for Gnostic Gospel, The Gospel of Mary; in chapter 13 "Role of Women in Gnosticism" on pp 128-130 for Gnostic Gospel, The Gospel of Mary; in chapter 15 "Politics of Power" on pp 145-147 for Gnostic Gospel, The Apocalypse of Peter; in chapter 17 "Monophysitism" on pp 163-164 for Gnostic Gospel, De Idolo Serapidis; in chapter 18 "Gnostics in the Crosshairs" on pp 166-167 for Gnostic Gospel, Bishop of Cyprus Epiphanius recounts an encounter with the Egyptian Gnostics

14. The Book of Jubilees; Little Genesis; translated by R. H. Charles; Pantianos Classics UK 1902; ISBN 978-197590-8164; for book identification: in chapter 7 "Essene"; in chapter 13 "Role of Women in Gnosticism"; and in chapter 16 "Nicene Creed"

15. The Books of Enoch; Complete Edition; translated by R.H. Charles; edited by Paul C. Schneiders; International Alliance Pro-Publishing USA 2012 Las Vegas Nevada; ISBN 978-1-60942-2004; for book identification: in chapter 7 "Essene"; in chapter 16 "Nicene Creed"; in chapter 23 "Children of the Law of One"

16. The City of God; author: St Augustine; Penguin books UK 1972; for book identification: in chapter 18 "Gnostics in the Crosshairs"

17. The Book of Job; King James Version of the Old Testament; text references appear in chapter 19 "Battleground of Doctrine" on page 186 for verse 22: 28

18. The travel logs of St Issa; author: Nicolas Roerich; book identification: in chapter 21 "Christ, the Traveler"

19. The Aquarian Gospel of Jesus the Christ; author: Levi H. Dowling; for book identification: in chapter 4 "Man, Apollonius"; in chapter 21 "Christ, the Traveler"; in chapter 22 "Mission of Yeshua"; text references appear in chapter 12 "Sin and Absolution" on pp 120-121 for Conversation with the Magi of

Persepolis, Egypt; in chapter 21 "Christ, the Traveler" on pp 201-202 for St Issa traveling in India; in chapter 21 "Christ, the Traveler" on pp 207-208 for Instruction from Salome in Hierapolis, Egypt; in chapter 21 "Christ, the Traveler" on pp 208-209 for The Sermon the Mount in Judea; in chapter 21 "Christ, the Traveler" on page 210 for meeting Vidyapati in India; in chapter 21 "Christ, the Traveler" on pp 210-211 for meeting Apollo and the oracle at Delphi in Greece

20. The Children of the Law of One and Lost teachings of Atlantis; author: Jon Peniel; Windsor Hills USA 1998; ISBN 978-096-6001532; for book identification: in chapter 1 "Argument"; chapter 7 "Essene"; in chapter 16 "Nicene Creed"; in chapter 21 "Christ, the Traveler"; in chapter 23 "Children of the Law of One"; in chapter 24 "Applying the Law of One"; in chapter 26 "Transition of the Ages"

21. Excerpts from Summa Theologica; author: St Thomas Aquinas; in chapter 27 "Conclusion" on pp 288-2

Other Books by Michael L. Kilday

Truth Never Changes: Earth Changes – 2009

ISBN-13: 978-0981947808

Truth Never Changes: The Genesis of the Path – 2011

ISBN-13: 978-1466279100

A Yippie's Lament – 2012

ISBN-13: 978-1475297737

Truth Never Changes: Conceiving a Spiritual Democracy - 2014

ISBN-13: 978-1500878429

No One Came Home From Woodstock - 2019

ISBN-13: 978-1727178128

www.ingramcontent.com/pod-product-compliance
Lightning Source LLC
Chambersburg PA
CBHW071251160426
43196CB00009B/1246